COLLECTED POEMS

Also by Allan Ahlberg

ALLAN AHLBERG

COLLECTED POEMS

Illustrated by Charlotte Voake

PUFFIN

PUFFIN BOOKS

Published by the Penguin Group
Penguin Books Ltd, 80 Strand, London WC2R 0RL, England
Penguin Group (USA) Inc., 375 Hudson Street, New York, New York 10014, USA
Penguin Group (Canada), 90 Eglinton Avenue East, Suite 700, Toronto, Ontario, Canada M4P 2Y3
(a division of Pearson Penguin Canada Inc.)
Penguin Ireland, 25 St Stephen's Green, Dublin 2, Ireland (a division of Penguin Books Ltd)
Penguin Group (Australia), 250 Camberwell Road, Camberwell, Victoria 3124, Australia
(a division of Pearson Australia Group Pty Ltd)
Penguin Books India Pvt Ltd, 11 Community Centre, Panchsheel Park, New Delhi – 110 017, India
Penguin Group (NZ), 67 Apollo Drive, Rosedale, North Shore 0632, New Zealand
(a division of Pearson New Zealand Ltd)
Penguin Books (South Africa) (Pty) Ltd, 24 Sturdee Avenue, Rosebank, Johannesburg 2196, South Africa

Penguin Books Ltd, Registered Offices: 80 Strand, London WC2R 0RL, England

puffinbooks.com

The poems in this collection are taken from:
Friendly Matches, first published by Viking 2001; published in Puffin Books 2002
Heard it in the Playground, first published by Viking Kestrel 1989; published in Puffin Books 1991
The Mighty Slide, first published by Viking 1988; published in Puffin Books 1989
Please Mrs Butler, first published by Kestrel Books 1983; published in Puffin Books 1984
The Mysteries of Zigomar © 1997 Allan Ahlberg; reproduced by
kind permission of Walker Books Ltd, London SE11 5HJ

This collection published 2008
1

Text copyright © Allan Ahlberg, 1983, 1988, 1989, 1997, 2001, 2008
Illustrations copyright © Charlotte Voake, 2008
Consultant designer: Douglas Martin

The moral right of the author and illustrator has been asserted

Set in 16/19 Rialto
Printed in Germany by Mohn Media

British Library Cataloguing in Publication Data
A CIP catalogue record for this book is available from the British Library

ISBN: 978–0–141–38259–3

www.greenpenguin.co.uk

Penguin Books is committed to a sustainable future
for our business, our readers and our planet.
The book in your hands is made from paper
certified by the Forest Stewardship Council.

Contents

I
Harrison's Desk

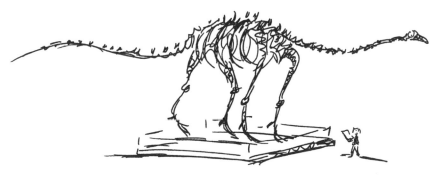

The Infants Do an Assembly
About Time

The infants
Do an assembly
About Time.

It has the past,
The present
And the future in it;

The seasons,
A digital watch,
And a six-year-old
Little old lady.

She gets her six-year-old
Family up
And directs them
Through the twenty-four hours
Of the day:

Out of bed
And – shortly after –
Back into it.
(Life does not stand still
In infant assemblies.)

The whole thing
Lasts for fifteen minutes.
Next week (space permitting):
Space.

Excuses

I've writ on the wrong page, Miss.
My pencil went all blunt.
My book was upside-down, Miss.
My book was back to front.

My margin's gone all crooked, Miss.
I've smudged mine with my scarf.
I've rubbed a hole in the paper, Miss.
My ruler's broke in half.

My work's blew out the window, Miss.
My work's fell in the bin.
The leg's dropped off my chair, Miss.
The ceiling's coming in.

I've ate a poison apple, Miss.
I've held a poison pen!
I think I'm being *kidnapped*, Miss!
So . . . can we start again?

Finishing Off

The teacher said:
Come here, Malcolm!
Look at the state of your book.
Stories and pictures unfinished
Wherever I look.

This model you started at Easter,
These plaster casts of your feet,
That graph of the local traffic –
All of them incomplete.

You've a half-baked pot in the kiln room
And a half-eaten cake in your drawer.
You don't even finish the jokes you tell –
I really can't take any more.

And Malcolm said
. . . very little.
He blinked and shuffled his feet.
The sentence he finally started
Remained incomplete.

He gazed for a time at the floorboards;
He stared for a while into space;
With an unlined, unwhiskered expression
On his unfinished face.

I See a Seagull

I see a seagull in the playground.
I see a crisp-bag and a glove;
Grey slides on the grey ice
And a grey sky above.

I see a white bird in the playground
And a pale face in the glass;
A room reflected behind me,
And the rest of the class.

I see a seagull in the playground.
I see it fly away.
A white bird in the grey sky:
The lesson for today.

Sale of Work

Who wants to buy:
Twenty sums, half right,
Two tracings of Francis Drake,
A nearly finished project on dogs
And a page of best handwriting?

Price reduced for quick sale:
Junk model of the Taj Mahal.
Delivery can be arranged.

What am I bid
For this fine old infant's newsbook
Complete with teacher's comments?

Hurry, hurry, hurry!
Brand-new paintings going cheap –
Still wet!

The Old Teacher

There was an old teacher
Who lived in a school,
Slept in the stock-cupboard as a rule,
With sheets of paper to make her bed
And a pillow of hymn-books
Under her head.

There was an old teacher
Who lived for years
In a Wendy house, or so it appears,
Eating the apples the children brought her,
And washing her face
In the goldfish water.

There was an old teacher
Who ended her days
Watching schools' TV and children's plays;
Saving the strength she could just about muster,
To powder her nose
With the blackboard duster.

There was an old teacher
Who finally died
Reading Ginn (Level One), which she couldn't abide.
The words on her tombstone said: TEN OUT OF TEN,
And her grave was the sandpit.
That's all now. Amen.

Harrison's Desk

There's something in Harrison's desk.
Put your ear against it and listen.
A noise like the chewing of pencils.

Harrison invites you to look inside.
He charges 5p a peep.
You lift the lid a little, and a little more . . .

A scritching, scratching somewhere at the back.
A noise like the chewing of rulers.
A peculiar movement.

There *is* something in Harrison's desk.
Harrison won't say what it is.
He says it sharpens his pencil sometimes.

He claims it helps him with his homework.
Then: a noise like an angry burp.
Look out, says Harrison, and slams the lid.

Harrison piles heavy objects on his desk.
You suspect a trick and watch him closely.
This sometimes happens, says Harrison.

A hole begins to appear in Harrison's desk.
A tiny hairy hand protrudes.
5p a peep, says Harrison, and covers it with his hat.

Harrison counts his 5p's.
You still suspect some sort of trick.
You prepare to ask for a refund.

The piled-up desk, meanwhile, begins to shake.
A stack of books collapses to the floor.
A hole appears in Harrison's hat.

Registration

Emma Hackett?
Here, Miss!
Billy McBone?
Here, Miss!
Derek Drew?
Here, Miss!
Margaret Thatcher?*
Still here, Miss!

Long John Silver?
Buccaneer, Miss!
Al Capone?
Racketeer, Miss!
Isambard Kingdom Brunel?
Engineer, Miss!
Davy Crockett?
Wild frontier, Miss!
Frank Bruno?
Cauliflower ear, Miss!

* Long-serving British prime minister (late twentieth century)

The White Rabbit?
Late, Miss!
Billy the Kid?
Infants, Miss!
Simple Simon?
Here . . . Sir.
Father Christmas?
Present (for you), Miss!

Count Dracula?
I, 2, 3, 4, Miss!
Necks door, Miss!
Dentist's!

The Invisible Man?
Nowhere, Miss!
Almighty God?
Everywhere, Miss!
Tarzan?
Aaaaaaaaaah! Miss.
Sleeping Beauty?
Zzz, Miss.

Do *a* Project

Do a project on dinosaurs.
Do a project on sport.
Do a project on the Empire State Building,
The Eiffel Tower,
The Blackpool Tower,
The top of a bus.

Ride a project on horses.
Suck a project on sweets.
Play a project on the piano.
Chop a project on trees
Down.

Write a project on paper,
A plaster cast,
The back of an envelope,
The head of a pin.

Write a project on the Great Wall of China,
Hadrian's Wall,
The playground wall,
Mrs Wall.

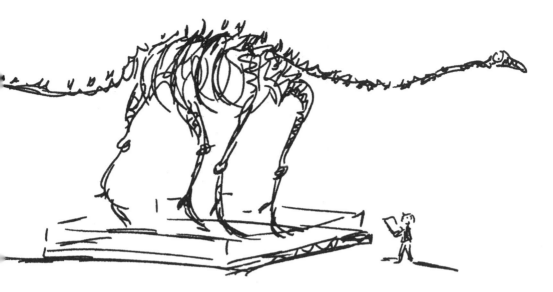

Do a project in pencil,
In ink,
In half an hour,
In bed,
Instead
of something else,
In verse,
Or worse –
Do a project in *playtime*.

Do a project on your hands and knees,
Your head,
With one arm tied behind you.

17

Do a project wearing handcuffs,
In a steel coffin,
Eighty feet down
At the bottom of the Hudson River
(Which ideally should be frozen over),
On Houdini.

Forget a project on Memory;
And refuse one on Obedience.

Not Now, Nigel

Not now, Nigel,
It's only half-past eight.
The school's not really open –
Your request will have to wait.

Not now, Nigel,
The register is due;
Some dinner-money's missing,
And I've got a headache too.

Not now, Nigel,
Can't you see I'm on my knees?
We're trying to find the hamster
(And I think I'm going to sneeze).

Not now, Nigel,
I'd like to hear your news,
But Alice isn't well –
She's just been sick all on my shoes.

Not now, Nigel,
Claire's bent her violin,
I ought to take a tablet
(And I *need* a double gin).

Not *here*, Nigel,
The staffroom's meant for us;
Your place is in the playground
(Or underneath a bus).

Not now, Nigel,
I still feel quite unwell;
And, furthermore, it's home time –
Off you go (saved by the bell).

Not . . . now, Nigel,
Though it's nice of you to call.
I'd love to ask you in
But there's a wolf-hound in the hall.

Not . . . now . . . Nigel,
It's really time for bed.
My temperature is rising –
There's a drum inside my head.

Tomorrow I'll feel better –
Tomorrow, wait and see.
But not now, Nigel.
The *nights* belong to me!

The Trial
of Derek Drew

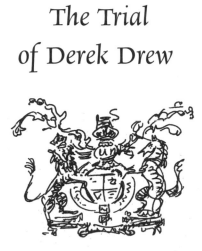

The charges

Derek Drew:
For leaving his reading book at home.
For scribbling his handwriting practice.
For swinging on the pegs in the cloakroom.
For sabotaging the girls' skipping.
For doing disgusting things with his dinner.

Also charged

Mrs Alice Drew (née Alice Jukes):
For giving birth to Derek Drew.
Mr Dennis Drew:
For aiding and abetting Mrs Drew.
Mrs Muriel Drew and Mr Donald Drew:
For giving birth to Dennis Drew, etc.
Mrs Jane Jukes and Mr Paul Jukes:
For giving birth to Alice Jukes, etc.
Previous generations of the Drew and Jukes families:
For being born, etc., etc.

Witnesses

'He's *always* forgetting his book.' Mrs Pine.
'He *can* write neatly, if he wants to.' Ditto.
'I seen him on the pegs, Miss!'
'And me!' 'And me!' Friends of the accused.
'He just kept jumpin' in the rope!' Eight third-year girls
In Miss Hodge's class.
'It was disgusting.' Mrs Foot (dinner-lady).

For *the defence*

'I was never *in* the cloakroom!' Derek Drew.

Mitigating circumstances

This boy is ten years old.
He asks for 386 other charges to be taken into consideration.
'He's not like this at home,' his mother says.

The *verdict*

Guilty.

The *sentence*

Life!
And do his handwriting again.

Small Quarrel

She didn't call for me as she usually does.
I shared my crisps with someone else.

I sat with someone else in assembly.
She gave me a funny look coming out.

I put a pencil mark on her maths book.
She put a felt-pen mark on mine.

She moved my ruler an inch.
I moved hers a centimetre.

I just touched her PE bag with my foot.
She put the smallest tip of her tongue out.

She dipped her paint brush in my yellow.
I washed mine in her paint water.

She did something too small to tell what it was.
I *pretended* to do something.

I walked home with her as usual.
She came to my house for tea.

Where's Everybody?

In the cloakroom
Wet coats
Quietly steaming.

In the office
Dinner-money
Piled in pounds.

In the head's room
Half a cup
Of cooling tea.

In the corridor
Cupboards
But no crowds.

In the hall
Abandoned
Apparatus.

In the classrooms
Unread books
And unpushed pencils.

In the infants
Lonely hamster
Wendy house to let;

Deserted Plasticine
Still waters
Silent sand.

In the meantime
In the playground . . .
A fire-drill.

The Mrs Butler Blues

I've got the
Teach-them-in-the-morning-
Playground-duty-
Teach-them-in-the-afternoon blues.
My head's like a drum;
My feet, cold and sore.
I'm feeling so glum;
Can't take any more.
I've got the
Teach-them-in-the-morning-
Playground-duty-
Teach-them-in-the-afternoon blues.

I've got the
Please-Miss-Tracey's-eating-
Where's-the-hamster?-
Miss-I've-broke-my-ruler blues.
My hair's full of chalk.
There's paint on my dress.
It hurts when I talk.
My handbag's a mess.
I've got the
Please-Miss-Tracey's-eating-
Where's-the-hamster?-
Miss-I've-broke-my-ruler blues.

I've got the
Teach-them-till-I'm-weary-
Parents'-evening-
Don't-get-home-till-midnight blues.
I know it's a job
That has to be done,
But I'd rather rob
A bank with a gun.
I've got the
Teach-them-till-I'm-weary-
Parents'-evening-
Don't-get-home-till-midnight blues.

One more time:
Teach-them-in-the-morning blues.
Hmm!
How'd you like to be in my . . . shoes?

2
Captain Jim

The History of
A Pair of Sinners

forgetting not their Ma who was one also

I. Wherein the Harrises and their Dishonest
  Trade are Introduced

In London Town some years ago
There dwelt a pair of sinners.
His name was Jack, her name was Belle
And they was baby-skinners.

They was brother and sister too
I should perhaps just add;
Lived with their Ma above the shop;
They hadn't got no dad.

Now baby-skinning, though a crime,
Weren't quite so bad as you'd suppose.
A skinner never hurt a child,
He only skinned him of his clothes.

Jack and Belle would work like this:
First, spy a posh new pram,
Distract the nursemaid from her task,
Then grab the child and scram.

Or else they'd lure some toddler
For him to roam and stray,
Then do him up inside Jack's coat
And smuggle him away.

One time they had a horse and cart
And, with a criminal lad,
They pinched a little schoolful;
The mistress weren't half mad.

Well, having got a child, y'see,
They'd skin him swift and neat,
Then leave him in his cotton drawers
A-shivering in the street.

Skinners, according to the police,
Most thrived when summer was gone.
The streets was gloomier places then,
And a child had more clothes on.

The shop which Mrs Harris kept,
That was their mother's name,
Sold baby clothes – I 'spect you guessed.
She was a crafty dame.

She washed 'n' ironed 'n' dyed the things
All colours under the sun.
She altered them with ribbons and such,
My word, she did have fun.

Then in the window they would go
Or on a tailor's rack.
Sometimes the folks they'd pinched things off
Come in and bought 'em back.

So, there y'are, that's Jack and Belle
And their dishonest trade.
And their dishonest mother too,
With a fortune being made.

Still, crime don't hardly ever pay;
Justice will lie in wait;
And how the Harrises met their end,
I'll now to you relate.

II. Wherein the Particulars of a Bad Business
   in St James's Park are Given

The season, it is winter;
The place, St James's Park;
The time, a quarter after four,
Just starting to get dark.

A nursemaid and her little charge
Are playing with a sledge.
They do not spot Jack Harris
A-crouched behind the hedge.

Now Belle gets talking to the maid
And asking her the way;
And while she points directions out
Her charge remains at play.

The child shouts, 'Whee!' as down he slides
Across the gleaming snow.
Until, that is, Jack grabs him,
And then he hollers, 'Oh!'

When she observes the empty sledge
And the fleeing figure of Jack,
The nursemaid says, 'That's torn it,
I 'spect I'll get the sack!'

Then with a start she recollects
Instructions she has had,
And takes a whistle from her bag
And blows the thing like mad.

Meanwhile, of course, the Harrises,
Having seen their plan succeed,
Are scooting off by different routes
To a place they have agreed.

Jack, for his part, is puffing hard
With the load he has to tote.
It ain't such easy work to run
With a infant up y'coat.

Nor it ain't so easy neither
Knowing best what course to steer
When the keepers of the park approach
And the constables appear.

But the police, at least, is busy
Taking statements from the maid
And pondering Jack's footprints
In the snow where they was laid.

The rendezvous is a shrubbery
Just in St James's Square.
When Jack arrives, exhausted like,
He finds Belle waiting there.

'Oh, Jack,' says Belle, as she regards
The luckless, pilfered child,
'We've got a little gold-mine here.
Look how his coat is styled!

'Look at his shirt and his little hat.
Look at this glove – it's kid!
And here, these boots – what beauties,
They must be worth a quid!'

The child, I'm happy to report,
Don't seem too much offended,
But stands a-sucking of his thumb
And hears hisself commended.

Jack, though, is worried, that is plain.
'Y'see,' he says to Belle,
'There is some funny business here;
I know it – I can tell.

'A whistle, well, that ain't so strange,
Nor coppers, come to that.
But when y'gets the Coldstream Guards
It's time to smell a rat!'

Jack was right – the guards was out,
And the Horse Artillery too.
The streets was teeming full of police,
It was a real to-do,

With shouts and lanterns in the square,
The tumult of trotting hoofs;
And watchmen searching houses,
Even climbing on the roofs.

Yet Belle keeps up her interest
In the child's sartorial charms,
Until upon his vest she spies
A certain coat-of-arms.

She spies it on his socks likewise.
Then in a voice of dread,
She says, 'Is your name . . . Bertie?'
The child, he nods his head.

'God bless my heart,' says Belle.
Her rosy cheek it pales.
'I think I know what's happened, Jack.
We've pinched the Prince of Wales!'

Which was the truth and did explain
The mighty hue and cry.
For there was halberdiers passing now,
And cannon rolling by.

'Well, knock me down with a feather,' says Jack.
'What a horrible, rotten trick.
Whoever would have thought it?
Here – get his clothes on quick!'

So Jack and Belle re-dress the Prince
And give his shoes a shine.
They're clumsy, as y'might expect:
Un-dressing's more their line.

Belle strikes a match to scrutinize
The small unflappable lad.
'He's tidier now than he was with his nurse,'
She says. 'That can't be bad.'

'What bothers me,' Jack Harris says,
'Is what to tell our mother.
I mean, see, skinning's one thing –
High treason, that's another.'

'Oh, don't say that,' Belle whispers.
'He'll get the wrong idea.'
She drops a curtsy to the Prince.
'Can I, er . . . speak to you, m'dear?

'Look here, Y'little Majesty,
This is a false alarm.
We are your loyalest subjects.
We never meant no harm.'

'No, just a joke,' says Jack,
'That's all what was intended.
You better toddle home now.
Your Ma might be offended.'

But Belle, from being truly loyal,
Won't hear of such a thing.
They cannot very well desert
The country's future king.

Besides, the Prince is disinclined
To leave the shrubbery.
It makes him think of Robin Hood,
And, 'I want to play,' says he.

Then for his sword he seizes up
A hefty piece of wood.
And waves it vigorously on high
Just like a outlaw should.

Thus, for a time, unwillingly,
The Harrises are stuck
With Belle in the role of Marian
And Jack as Friar Tuck.

While the little Prince in wild delight
Goes charging here and there,
A-bossing of his men about
And saving his lady fair.

'Be careful with y'sword, my liege,'
Says Belle, provoked to speak.
'You bang my brother's head like that,
He'll be in bed for a week!'

'Not only – aargh! – that,' shouts Jack,
As he suffers a clout again.
'Why fight with me at all?
I'm one of his Merrie – aargh! – Men.'

Belle says, 'Hush up there, do;
You'll give us all away.'
'Hush up y'self,' Jack mutters.
'It's me he's trying to slay.'

Presently the Prince gets fagged
From all the rogues he's smote,
And says it is his wish to ride
Inside Jack Harris's coat.

I expect this was a novel thing
For so well-raised a lad.
It's doubtful if he got the chance
When he was with his dad.

Though sulking yet from previous hurts
And mindful of further blows,
Jack buttons up the royal boy
Till not a hair of him shows.

By now, of course, it is quite dark.
Snow has begun to fall.
The weary Prince is dozing off.
Belle covers her head with a shawl.

'Let's risk it and smuggle him back,' says she.
'Just up to the palace gate.'
She clutches her shawl. 'Be a patriot, Jack!
Come on, it's getting late.'

Jack weighs this up for a minute.
He has a look in the square.
The snow is thick and swirling.
There hardly seems nobody there.

'Right-o,' says he. 'I ever was
A tender-hearted man.'
He takes Belle's arm; they ventures forth.
'Look nonchalant, if y' can.'

Out from the square the Harrises trot
Into a narrow street.
They hear the cry of a bellman;
The tramp of muffled feet.

A coster-lady calls to them
From the steps of a hotel.
'Bad business this, about the Prince!'
'Oh, terrible,' says Belle.

A chimney-sweeper hurries by,
The snow piled on his hat.
'You've heard the news?' 'We have,' says Jack.
'Who'd do a thing like that?'

At last they come into the Mall.
The Prince is still a-snoozing.
'We're winning, Jack,' his sister says.
Then, lo and behold, they're losing.

The snow, it suddenly abates.
A street lamp lights the scene.
A chilly fear invests Belle's heart
Where her warm hopes had been.

Now up the Mall a carriage drives,
Its springs and harness jigging.
Inside, the nursemaid looking peeved;
The Queen has give her a wigging,

And sent her off to join the search.
The maid stares mournfully out;
Claps eyes on the approaching Jack
And gives a grateful shout.

'That's him – look, there – and her likewise!'
The carriage skids to a halt.
Whistles and bugles rend the air.
Says Belle, 'It's all my fault.'

Meanwhile, the little sleeping Prince,
Roused by the hullabaloo,
Protrudes his head out of Jack's coat
Like the son of a kangaroo.

'Pity we never brought his sword,'
Says Jack, by way of a quip.
'He could've smacked a few of their heads
While you and me give 'em the slip.'

For Jack well knows the jig is up.
No man should hope to flee;
Not when he's getting cornered
By the Household Cavalry.

Soon from the park a mighty horde
Of constables appear,
And boldly cry, 'Hallo, hallo,
Now then, what's going on here?'

'I doubt if you'll believe this, sirs,'
Says the perspiring Jack;
'But this child was took erroneously.
We was just bringing him back.'

'A likely tale, my shifty lad,'
The officers reply.
'You'll tell us next you're Robin Hood.'
'Oh, no,' says Jack. 'Not I.'

III. *Wherein the Scene of this History is Closed*

The trial of all the Harrises
(Their Ma got nabbed as well)
Took place at the Old Bailey
As I shall briefly tell.

To avoid the charge of treason,
What they found they had to do
Was own up to their actual crime
And more or less prove it too.

Thus, a crowd of little infants
Was called and took the oath,
Swore Jack and Belle had skinned 'em
And recognized them both.

The nursemaid gave her evidence,
And the sledge – Exhibit A –
Was held aloft in the courtroom
For the jury to survey.

The royal Prince did not appear.
He had been sent to bed
For applying his father's walking-stick
To a elderly footman's head.

'But you also claim it was a joke,'
Said the judge to the accused.
'Well, I'll tell you this for nothing.
The Queen was not amused.'

Then he sentenced them to go to jail
For a couple of years apiece,
And hoped that when they was let out
Their criminal ways would cease.

And cease they did, it can be said,
For now the Harrises keep
A pet shop in the Brompton Road:
BEST DOGS AND BUDGIES — CHEEP!

Postscript

Unfortunately, I have just heard,
While the above was being wrote,
Jack was seen leaving London Zoo
With a parrot up his coat.

Belle Harris had distracted
The keeper and his men.
I fear the pair of 'em has gone back
To sinning once again.

HISTORICAL NOTE

Child Stripping – This is generally done by females, old debauched drunken hags who watch their opportunity to accost children passing in the streets, tidily dressed with good boots and clothes. They entice them away to a low or quiet neighbourhood for the purpose, as they say, of buying them sweets, or with some other pretext. When they get into a convenient place, they give them a halfpenny or some sweets, and take off the articles of dress, and tell them to remain till they return, when they go away with the booty.

This is done most frequently in mews in the West-end, and at Clerkenwell, Westminster, the Borough, and other similar localities. These heartless debased women sometimes commit these felonies in the disreputable neighbourhoods where they live, but more frequently in distant places, where they are not known and cannot be easily traced. This mode of felony is not so prevalent in the metropolis as formerly. In most cases, it is done at dusk in the winter evenings, from 7 to 10 o'clock.

From Henry Mayhew's
London Labour and the London Poor,
Vol. IV (published 1862)

Captain Jim

You've heard the tales of Tarzan,
Chinese Charlie Chan,
Sherlock Holmes of Baker Street
And 'cow pie' Desperate Dan;
Well, now I'm going to tell you
Of another kind of man.

Yes, now I'm going to tell you,
As the light grows dim,
And we sit here in the jungle
At the wide world's rim,
Of the man who matched them all:
And his name was Captain Jim.

Where he came from is a mystery,
Where he went to no one knows,
But his talents were amazing
(From his eyebrows to his toes!),
And his brain was full of brainwaves,
And his reputation grows.

It all began one summer
Near this very spot,
When the river-boats were steaming
And the river banks were hot,
And the *crocodiles* were teeming,
Which sometimes a child forgot.

I was playing with my brothers,
Bertie, Joe and little Frank,
In the mangrove trees that twisted
From that mossed and muddy bank;
When young Frank climbed out too far,
Slipped and fell, and straightways – sank.

Hardly had he hit the water,
Barely had the ripples spread,
When the river started foaming
And we saw with awful dread
Half a dozen snapping snouts
In a hurry to be fed.

Well, we shouted and we threw things,
Lumps of rock and bits of wood,
And young Frank, he cried for help
And tried to swim as best he could,
But the crocs were closing in
And it wasn't any good.

Then at last when all seemed lost,
And it was looking grim,
There was a *blur* beside us,
And a man leapt in to swim
Like an arrow from a bow:
And his name was Captain Jim.

He was dressed, we later noticed,
In a suit of gleaming white,
And he even had his hat on;
Oh, it was a stirring sight,
As he surged into the fray
Like a charge of dynamite.

With his bare hands and a cricket bat
He gave the crocs what for;
Hit the six of them for six,
Though I doubt they kept the score.
Then he gave a tow to little Frank
And calmly swam to shore.

And that was the beginning,
The first time he was seen,
In the heat and haze of summer
When the air itself was green
And the river banks were steaming . . .
And he chose to intervene.

Where he came from is a mystery,
Why he stayed we never knew,
But he took a room at Macey's
And he moored his own canoe
At the wharf beside the warehouse.
And he bought a cockatoo.

Now this, I should remind you,
Was twenty years ago,
In nineteen thirty-one,
When the pace of life was slow,
And Grandpa ran the Copper Mine
And built this bungalow.

And the town was smaller then,
Just some houses and a pier,
And the Steamship Company Office
With a barber's at the rear,
And a visiting policeman
Who came by four times a year.

So it took no time at all
For the tale to get about;
How the stranger with a cricket bat
Had fished young Frankie out,
And hammered *fourteen* crocodiles
With one enormous clout.

And as the weeks went by,
There were other tales to tell:
How he saved the Baxters' baby
(With the speed of a gazelle!)
And the Baxters' baby's teddy –
It was needing help as well.

How he stopped a charging warthog
As it rampaged through the town
(Knocking bikes and fences flying,
Pulling wires and washing down),
With a matadorial flourish
And a matadorial frown.

Well, we followed him about, of course,
Or watched him where he sat
On Macey's back verandah
In his dazzling suit and hat,
With a glass of tea beside him,
And – sometimes – Macey's cat.

We listened to the gossip
Inside the barber's shop.
Some said he was a gambler,
Some said he was a cop,
And oaths were sworn and bets were laid
On just how long he'd stop.

We eavesdropped on the talk
Outside the General Store.
They marvelled at his manicure
And at the clothes he wore.
Whoever did his laundry?
What was that cricket bat for?

In time the summer ended;
The rains began to fall;
Moss clung to the houses
And creepers covered all.
The river was a torrent
And the grass grew eight feet tall.

And still he lived among us
And continued to amaze,
With his quick, explosive actions,
And his steady *brainy* gaze;
Though he gave no thought to wages,
And he never looked for praise.

And he showed us how to wrestle,
And he taught us how to dive,
And he saved us from the wild bees –
We had blundered on a hive –
When he walloped it to safety
With a perfect cover drive.

He delivered Mrs Foster's fourth,
When Doc Gains fell down drunk.
(The doctor diagnosed himself:
'I'm drunker than a skunk!')
Then Captain Jim took care of *him*,
And tucked him in his bunk.

At Christmas, when a touring troupe
Arrived to do a show,
And the tenor caught a fever
And it was touch-and-go,
Who was it calmly took his place?
Well, I expect you know.

And so the seasons passed,
And the months became a year,
And he saved us from a cheetah,
And he bought us ginger beer,
And he taught us how to make our own . . .
And when to interfere.

He said: the world's a puzzle,
A game of keys and locks;
A mirror in a mirror,
A box within a box;
And we must do the best we can
And stand up to the shocks.

He told us: that's the moral,
In a world without a plan,
In a world without a meaning,
Designed to puzzle man;
You must do your intervening
In the best way that you can.

Some said he was a writer,
And some, a diplomat;
A traveller, spy, geologist,
And various things like that.
We said he was a cricketer;
How else explain the bat?

'You'd been on tour,' said little Frank.
'And scored a ton,' said Joe.
'And when the boat returned to home,'
Said I, 'you didn't go.'
But when we asked him was it true,
He said, 'Well . . . yes and no.'

And he built a bridge that summer,
And he made a mighty kite,
And he saved us from the axeman,
Who was 'axing' for a fight,
And he beat the Mayor at poker,
And he caught quail in the night.

He read the weeks-old papers,
And played the gramophone,
And climbed the hills above the town,
And watched the sky alone,
And taught the barber's daughter chess
(Who's now your Auntie Joan).

Then, one evening in September,
As we sat up on the pier,
With our mango-chutney sandwiches
And home-made ginger beer,
And our Steamboat Billy comics . . .
We saw him disappear.

In his suit of gleaming white
And his loaded-up canoe,
He passed quickly out of sight,
There was nothing we could do,
He had paid his bill at Macey's;
And he took the cockatoo.

Well, we shouted from the quayside
And we ran along the bank,
And scrambled in the mangroves,
Delayed by little Frank;
But he was gone for evermore,
And left behind . . . a blank.

Yet not quite a blank, perhaps,
For he did leave us a note
And some marbles (c/o Macey's),
And this is what he wrote:
'Watch out for life's crocodiles,
And try to stay afloat.'

Why he came remained a mystery,
Why he left us, no one knows,
But his talents were amazing
(From his eyebrows to his toes!),
And though it's now all history,
Still his reputation grows:

The voice of Nelson Eddy,
The dash of Errol Flynn,
The brains of Albert Einstein,
The speed of Rin Tin Tin,
The cover drive of Bradman,
The pluck of Gunga Din.

That's how we have remembered,
As the years grow dim
And life slips slowly by
On the wide world's rim,
The man who matched them all:
And his name was Captain Jim.

Now little Frank is bigger,
And Bertie's married Joan,
And Joe's become an engineer
With 'Wireless-Telephone',
And I tell bedtime stories
To children of my own.

One final thing, before I go
(I heard your mother call);
A few years back, it must have been,
When you were both quite small,
I bought some cigarette cards
At the Monday Market Stall.

Woodbine's Famous Cricketers,
Fifty in the set;
They were faded, creased and dog-eared,
Badly stained with dust and sweat;
Yet there was a face among them
That I never could forget.

It was him all right, I'd swear it;
It was him without a doubt,
With his bat raised in a flourish
Letting go a mighty clout.
'Captain James Fitz . . . (blur),' it stated:
'Four-forty-nine not out.'

The Goals of Bingo Boot

The fans in the stands are silent
You could hear the fall of a pin
For the fabulous game just ended
And the tale that's about to begin.

In nineteen hundred and twenty-two
A little boy was born
His baby cot was second-hand
His baby shawl was torn.
He had no teeth or teddy bear
His hair was incomplete
But he was the possessor of
The most amazing feet.

When Bingo Boot was two years old
He chewed his little crust
His poor old dad was on the dole
His poor old pram was bust.
Yet Bingo wasn't worried
Though his baby feet would itch
And he could hardly wait till
He could stroll – out on the pitch.

In school young Bingo languished
At the bottom of the class
His ball control was good
It was exams he couldn't pass.
His little pals all shouted, 'Foul!'
And tended to agree
If only teachers tested feet
He'd get a Ph.D.

And all the while in streets and parks
On pitches large or small
Without a proper pair of boots
Sometimes without a ball!
With tin cans in the clattering yard
In weather cold or hot
Young Bingo shimmied left and right
And scored with every shot.

His poor old mum scrubbed office floors
His poor old gran did too
The pantry was an empty place
The rent was overdue.
Then Bingo had a brainwave
Shall I tell you what he did?
He sold himself to the Arsenal
For thirteen thousand quid.

The first game that he ever played
At the tender age of ten
Young Bingo just ran rings round
Eleven baffled men.
The fans of course went crazy
The fans went, 'Ooh!' and 'Ah!'
While Bingo took the match ball home
And bought his dad a car.

And so the years went flying by
In liniment and sweat
Life was a great high-scoring game
An ever-bulging net
And Arsenal won the cup and league
Six seasons on the trot
All on account of Bingo Boot
And his most amazing shot.

But now the storm clouds gathered
And at last the whistle blew
For the start of a really *crucial* game
The battle of World War Two.
It was England versus Germany
And Bingo heard the call
He marched away in his shooting boots
To assist in Adolf's fall.

Then when the war was finished
And he'd left the fusiliers
Brave Bingo served the Gunners
For another fifteen years.
No net was ever empty
No sheet was ever clean
He scored more goals a season
Than even Dixie Dean.

His goals in life were modest though
He had no wish to be
Sir Bingo Boot of Camden Town
Or Bingo O.B.E.
He loved his wife and family
His kiddies, Joyce and Jim,
He never went to see the King
The King came to see him.

His twilight years were mostly spent
With a ball in the local park
Kicking about with the local team
Having a laugh and a lark.
Yet still they couldn't stop him
His old swerve worked a treat
Till he died at last with his boots on
Those most amazing feet.

Eyes down for Bingo (in his grave)
The final whistle blown
The fans rolled up from miles around
'You'll never walk alone!'
While Bingo's spirit shimmied
With all its usual grace.
And then was . . . relegated
To a most appalling place.

The Devil sat in his chairman's chair
And spoke in Bingo's ear
'I've pulled a few strings, I must confess,
To arrange your transfer here.
For we've got this little match, y'see
(And I've got this little bet)
Away to the Heavenly City
And we've never beaten them yet.'

The Heavenly City were quite a side
(With fans who could *really* sing)
Cherubs and seraphs in the squad
And angels on the wing.
St Paul was a rock at centre half
St Elvis a rock 'n' roll
They had Mother Teresa to captain the team
And Almighty God in goal.

The kick-off time was three o'clock
At the City's heavenly ground
The angels of the Lord came down
And passed the ball around.
The tackles started flying
Nero fouled a nun
And the ref booked Good King Wenceslas
For a trip on Attila the Hun.

The Hades fans were howling
'We're the boys from Beelzebub!'
While God took Charlie Chaplin off
And brought Jesus on as a sub.
The second half went racing by
The pace was faster still
There was less than a minute left to play
And the score remained nil–nil.

Then Bingo dribbled round St Mark
Who never had a prayer
Left frail St Francis on his knees
And danced past Fred Astaire.
The goal was at his mercy now
It seemed he couldn't fail
When – bang! – a tackle from behind
From Florence Nightingale.

A penalty! The crowd was stunned.
The Devil's lot gave thanks,
Though God in goal, the angels cried,
Was as good as Gordon Banks.
A cruel choice for Bingo
Whatever should he do
Be false to his god-given gifts
Or give the Devil his due?

Even God had a frown on His face
And powerful reasons to pray.
If I let this in, He told Himself
There'll be the Devil to pay.
Now Bingo stepped up with the ball
And placed it on the spot
Stepped back, breathed deep, ran calmly in
Then shimmied left . . . and shot.

*

In nineteen hundred and twenty-two
A little boy was born
His baby cot was second-hand
His baby shawl was torn.
Who would have guessed that at the end
This tiny tot would be
The one who beat Almighty God
With the perfect penalty?

No goalie could have saved that shot
No God or Holy Ghost
But it went where Bingo placed it
And hit the holy post,
Rebounded like a rocket
To Marie Antoinette
Who skipped up to the other end
And slammed it in the net.

The fans in the stands went barmy
City had won one–nil.
The Devil stayed down in his dugout
Defeat was a bitter pill.
Till God came along with an offer
Quite genuine and real
To forget their bet and agree instead
On a little . . . transfer deal.

So Bingo rose to Heaven
Up to the Pearly Gate.
'The boy done good!' St Peter cried
'The boy done great!'
And there he lives . . . forever
His goals in life complete
That sainted soccer player
With the most amazing feet.

The fans in the stands are leaving
As fast as their wings will allow
They think that the story's over
    It is now.

3
The Actor's Mother

Why Must We Go to School?

Why must we go to school, dad?
Tell us, dear daddy, do.
Give us your thoughts on this problem, please;
No one knows better than you.

To prepare for life, my darling child,
Or so it seems to me;
And stop you all from running wild –
Now, shut up and eat your tea!

Why must we go to school, dad?
Settle the question, do.
Tell us, dear daddy, as much as you can;
We're really relying on you.

To learn about fractions and Francis Drake,
I feel inclined to say,
And give your poor mother a bit of a break –
Now, push off and go out to play!

Why must we go to school, daddy?
Tell us, dear desperate dad.
One little hint, that's all we ask –
It's a puzzle that's driving us mad.

To find all the teachers something to do,
Or so I've heard it said,
And swot up the questions your kids'll ask you,
My darlings – now, buzz off to bed!

Polite Children

May we have our ball, please
May we have it back?
We never meant to lose it
Or give it such a whack.

It shot right past the goalie
It shot right past the goal
And really then what happened next
Was out of our control.

It truly was such rotten luck
For all concerned that you
Were halfway up a ladder
When the ball came flying through.

We also very much regret
What happened to your cat
It's tragic when an animal
Gets landed on like that.

Your poor wife too we understand
Was pretty much upset
When phoning for the doctor
And phoning for the vet,

She quite forgot the oven.
It simply is no joke
When your husband's half unconscious
And your house is full of smoke.

The fire-brigade, of course, meant well
It wasn't their mistake
That there was no fire to speak of
Just a bit of well-done steak.

Still clouds have silver linings
And pains are soon forgot
While your lawn will surely flourish
From the hosing that it got.

The game of life is never lost
The future's not all black
And the ball itself seems quite unmarked.
So . . . may we have it back?

Lullaby for a Referee's Baby

The pitch is cold and dark
The night is dark and deep
The players all have gone to bed
So sleep, baby, sleep.

The whistle's on the shelf
The boots are in a heap
The kit is in the laundry bag
So sleep, baby, sleep.

The house is warm and dark
The stairs are dark and steep
And Daddy's here beside your cot
To send you off . . . to sleep.

Bags I

Bags I the dummy
Bags I the cot
Bags I the rubber duck
That other baby's got.

Bags I the cricket ball
Wickets and bat
Bags I the hamster
Bags I the cat.

Bags I the pop records
Hear the music throb
Bags I the A levels
Bags I the job.

Bags I the sweetheart
Lovers for life
Bags I the husband
Bags I the wife.

Bags I the savings
The mortgage and then
Bags I the baby –
Here we go again!

Bags I not the glasses
The nearly bald head
Bags under eyes
And the middle-aged spread.

Bags I the memories
How it all began
Bags I the grandpa
Bags I the gran.

Bags I the hearing-aid
Bags I the stick
Bags I the ending
Quiet and quick.

Goodbye world!
Goodbye me!
Bags I the coffin
RIP.

I Did a Bad Thing Once

I did a bad thing once.
I took this money from my mother's purse
For bubble gum.
What made it worse,
She bought me some
For being good, while I'd been vice versa
So to speak – that made it worser.

Father and Child

Upon that sharp and frosty eve
Muffled in scarf and glove
With frosty snow beneath their feet
And frosty sky above:
A father and his child.

Climbing the narrow hilly street
With letters in their hands
And Christmas cards and packets too
To where the postbox stands.
The child runs on ahead.

A cautious car comes ghosting by
An ebb and flow of light.
Somewhere an ice-cream van chimes out –
Ice-cream on such a night!
The child, though, would like one.

The father raises up his face
He stares into the sky
And marvels at the myriad stars
And hears his child reply:
It's like a join-the-dots.

Back down the hill, now hand-in-hand
Father and child return
While overhead and unobserved
The frosty heavens burn.
And the child thinks: Ice-cream!

Lost

Dear Mrs Butler, this is just a note
About our Raymond's coat
Which he came home without last night,
So I thought I'd better write.

He was minus his scarf as well, I regret
To say; and his grandma is most upset
As she knitted it and it's pure
Wool. You'll appreciate her feelings, I'm sure.

Also, his swimming towel has gone
Out of his PE bag, he says, and one
Of his socks too – it's purplish and green
With a darn in the heel. His sister Jean

Has a pair very similar. And while
I remember, is there news yet of those fairisle
Gloves which Raymond lost that time
After the visit to the pantomime?

Well, I think that's all. I will close now,
Best wishes, yours sincerely, Maureen Howe
(Mrs). P.S. I did once write before
About his father's hat that Raymond wore

In the school play and later could not find,
But got no reply. Still, never mind,
Raymond tells me now he might have lost the note,
Or left it in the pocket of his coat.

Getting Up for School

I'm getting up for school
Getting up for school
Getting, getting
Up for, up for
Soft-boiled egg and steamy cup for
Getting up for school.

I'll soon be up for school
Soon be up for school
Soon be leaping
Striding (creeping!)
Bye-bye boring beds and sleeping
Out and off to school.

I'm nearly up for school
Nearly up for school
Nearly (really!)
Out of bed for
Rise and shine your sleepy head for
Leave that snug and steamy bed for
Steamy, dreamy soft-boiled bed for
Bed for, bed for . . .

Won't be long now
Get – get – getting
In a minute
Up – up – up
Just a jiffy . . . Ah! (*yawn*)
For school.

Our Mother

Our mother is a detective.
She is a great finder of clues.
She found the mud and grass on our shoes,
When we were told not to go in the park –
Because it would be getting dark –
But come straight home.

She found the jam on our thumbs,
And in our beds the tiniest crumbs
From the cakes we said we had not eaten.
When we blamed the cat for breaking the fruit bowl –
Because we did not want any fuss –
She *knew* it was us.

Things I Have Been Doing Lately

Things I have been doing lately:
Pretending to go mad
Eating my own cheeks from the inside
Growing taller
Keeping a secret
Keeping a worm in a jar
Keeping a good dream going
Picking a scab on my elbow
Rolling the cat up in a rug
Blowing bubbles in my spit
Making myself dizzy
Holding my breath
Pressing my eyeballs so that I become temporarily blind
Being very nearly ten
Practising my signature . . .

Saving the best till last.

The Actor's Mother

No charming chatty Prince for him,
Lines by the yard.
He mostly stands there with a spear:
My son, the guard.

He never plays the Captain's part,
Always the crew.
'Aye, aye!' he cries, occasionally.
His lines are few.

He doesn't get the better roles,
Takes after me.
Sometimes he never speaks at all:
My son, the tree.

The only time he got some lines,
Just half a page,
He had to shout them through a door,
Invisibly – offstage!

Still, curtains fall eventually,
And homeward in the car
His dad and I can then admire:
Our son, the star.

Bedtime

When I go upstairs to bed,
I usually give a loud cough.
This is to scare The Monster off.

When I come to my room,
I usually slam the door right back.
This is to squash The Man in Black
Who sometimes hides there.

Nor do I walk to the bed,
But usually run and jump instead.
This is to stop The Hand –
Which is under there all right –
From grabbing my ankles.

4
Billy McBone

Where I Sit Writing

Where I sit writing I can see
A page, a pen, a line or three
Of scribbled verse; a cup of tea.

A spider's web, a window pane,
A garden blurred a bit with rain,
A low and leaden sky; a plane.

Where I sit writing I can see
An evening sky, a sodden tree,
A window pane reflecting . . . me.

Out in the garden's fading light,
Departing day, approaching night,
He copies every word I write.

Where I sit writing I can see
A hand, a pen, a verse or three;
A distant road; a cup – no tea.

A list of rhymes, some crossings out,
Confusions, choices, doodles, doubt.
No clue to what it's all about.

Where I sit writing I can see
A glowing sky, a darkened tree,
Some Sellotape, a saucer . . . me.

The Boy Without a Name

I remember him clearly
And it was thirty years ago or more:
A boy without a name.

A friendless, silent boy,
His face blotched red and flaking raw,
His expression, infinitely sad.

Some kind of eczema
It was, I now suppose,
The rusty iron mask he wore.

But in those days we confidently swore
It was from playing near dustbins
And handling broken eggshells.

His hands, of course, and knees
Were similarly scabbed and cracked and dry.
The rest of him we never saw.

They said it wasn't catching: still, we knew
And strained away from him along the corridor,
Sharing a ruler only under protest.

I remember the others: Brian Evans,
Trevor Darby, Dorothy Cutler.
And the teachers: Mrs Palmer, Mr Waugh.

I remember Albert, who collected buttons,
And Amos, frothing his milk up with a straw.
But *his* name, no, for it was never used.

I need a time-machine.
I must get back to nineteen fifty-four
And play with him, or talk, at least.

For now I often wake to see
His ordinary, haunting face, his flaw.
I hope his mother loved him.

Oh, children, don't be crueller than you need.
The faces that you spit on or ignore
Will get you in the end.

The Slow Man

The phone rings
But never long enough
For the Slow Man.

By the time
The set's switched on
His favourite programme's over.

His tea grows cold
From cup to lip,
His soup evaporates.

He laughs, eventually,
At jokes long since
Gone out of fashion.

Sell-by dates
And limited special offers
Defeat him.

He comes home
With yesterday's paper
And reads it . . . tomorrow.

The Filling Station
(country style)

The word is spreadin' across the nation,
Git your kids to the Fillin' Station.
Teachers now can take their ease
While moms and dads say, 'Fill 'em up, please!'

Fill 'em up with Maths and Readin'.
Anythin' more, Ma'am, you'll be needin'?
Spanish, German, History?
Half a dozen subjects and y'get one free.

Attach these wires to your wrist,
Relax here on this special bed,
Shut y'eyes and don't resist,
Feel that education flowin' into your head.

*

C'mon down to the Fillin' Station,
We're gonna build a new generation.
How 'bout the toddler? Only three?
Soon he'll be a little infant prodigy.

Forget about your sand 'n' water,
Teach him all those things y'oughter.
Shakespeare, Dickens, Roald Dahl too;
Literature is good for you.

Place these goggles over his eyes,
Lay him in this little cot,
Golden slumbers, big surprise,
When he wakes up, he'll know the lot.

*

In one ear and in the other.
Could y'use a top-up for his older brother?
Seems a bit empty, if'n you ask me.
Have y'ever thought about a PhD?

No more learnin', no more books,
No more tough exams to pass.
No more teachers' grumpy looks,
Soon we'll *all* be top of the class.

*

Just got back from the Fillin' Station,
We're gonna have a big celebration.
Kids all sittin' in a row,
Ain't a blessed thing that they don't know.

Name that wind in the south of France.
What's the square of minus eight?
Is it true that bees can dance?
Who wrote a show called *Kiss Me Kate*?
Where do whales and penguins thrive?
What's the longest river in Tennessee?
Will the human race survive . . .?
Y'all know the answers – and so do we!

Yippee!

The word is spreadin' across the nation,
Git your kids to the Fillin' Station.
Collect them tokens, don't be dumb;
Albert Einstein, here – we – come!

Scabs

The scab on Jean's knee
Is geographical.
Bexhill-on-Sea:
Tripped up on school trip.

The scab on Henry's knee
Is historical.
Oldest scab in Class Three:
Second year sack race.

The scab on Paul's knee
Is pugilistical.
Fighting Clive Key:
He got a cut lip.

The scab on Sally's knee
Is psychological.
Hurts if she does PE:
Painless at playtime.

The scab on Brian's knee
Is bibliographical.
Fooling around in library:
Banged into bookcase.

The scabs on the twins' knees
Are identical.
Likewise the remedies:
Hankies and spit.

The scab on Eric's knee
Is economical.
£2.50:
Second-hand skates.

The scab on Debby's knee
Is diabolical.
Nothing to see:
Hurts like the devil.

Worlds

The first world
Was made of paper.
God screwed it up in a ball.
It would not do at all.

The second world
Was made of ice-cream,
Fudge flavour mostly,
In a delicate (8000-mile diameter) wafer cup.
God ate it up.

The third world
Was made of modelling clay.
God baked it in the oven
And gave it to his grandma.

The ninth world
Was made of house bricks,
Artfully arranged.
God won second prize
In a competition with it.

The twelfth world
Was made – woven, actually –
Of magic-carpet material.
It commuted between here and there.
There were two billion
Uncomplicated if somewhat wind-blown
People on it.

The thirteenth world
Was perfect.
God put it down somewhere
And has been looking for it
Ever since.

The twenty-fifth world
Was made of a miraculous new substance
With mind-boggling properties.
It had an unfortunate smell, though,
Like rarely opened wardrobes.

The thirtieth world
Was made of dirt and water
Day and night
Grass
Trees
Bungalows
Odd socks
Incomplete jigsaw puzzles
Volcanoes
Fluff
Happiness and boredom
Wedding rings
General elections
Telephone books
And me and you.

God said that it would do.

Boys

Boys will be boys
But before that
They sit around in prams
In woolly hats
With sticky chins
Waiting.

Boys who used to be boys
(i.e. *old* boys)
On the other hand
Sit around in pubs
Or on the upper decks of buses
With stubbly chins
Remembering.

Boys who *are* boys
Meanwhile
Just get on with it.

It is a Puzzle

My friend
Is not my friend any more.
She has secrets from me
And goes about with Tracy Hackett.

I would
Like to get her back,
Only do not want to say so.
So I pretend
To have secrets from her
And go about with Alice Banks.

But what bothers me is,
Maybe *she* is pretending
And would like *me* back,
Only does not want to say so.

In which case
Maybe it bothers her
That *I* am pretending.

But if we are both pretending,
Then really we are friends
And do not know it.

On the other hand,
How can we be friends
And have secrets from each other
And go about with other people?

My friend
Is not my friend any more,
Unless she is pretending.
I cannot think what to do.
It is a puzzle.

Sometimes God

Sometimes when I'm in trouble,
Like if Gary Hubble
And his gang
Are going to get me and beat me up,
Or I'm outside Mr Baggot's door
Waiting to have the slipper for pour-
Ing paint water in Glenis Parker's shoe,
This is what I do:
I ask for help from God.

Get me out of this, God, I say.
I'll behave myself then –
Every day.

Sometimes when I'm really
Scared, like once when I nearly
Got bit by this horse,
Or the other
Week when Russell Tucker's brother
Was going to beat me up
For throwing Russell Tucker's PE bag
On the boiler-house roof, or Roy
And me got caught in the toi-
Lets by Mr Baggot turning all the taps on
And he said,
I've had enough of boys like you,
This is what I do:
I ask for help from God.

Stop this happening, God, I say.
I'll believe in You then –
Every day.

And it works . . . sometimes.

Billy McBone

Billy McBone
Had a mind of his own,
Which he mostly kept under his hat.
The teachers all thought
That he couldn't be taught,
But Bill didn't seem to mind that.

Billy McBone
Had a mind of his own,
Which the teachers had searched for for years.
Trying test after test,
They still never guessed
It was hidden between his ears.

Billy McBone
Had a mind of his own,
Which only his friends ever saw.
When the teacher said, 'Bill,
Whereabouts is Brazil?'
He just shuffled and stared at the floor.

Billy McBone
Had a mind of his own,
Which he kept under lock and key.
While the teachers in vain
Tried to burgle his brain,
Bill's thoughts were off wandering free.

Balls on the Roof

The caretaker went on the roof today,
The first time for years.
He put his ladder against the wall
And cleared the guttering.

Some of the children stayed to watch;
It was after school.
He threw the balls down that he found
And they caught them.

That guttering was a graveyard for balls.
Balls with moss on them.
Balls you couldn't even buy any more.
Balls too old to bounce.

There was a sorbo ball with R.T. on it,
Not Russell Tucker's –
Raymond Tate's – he'd left – ages ago!
Gone to the Comp.

There was a ball so perished and worn,
It was like Aero.
I could've kicked that up, the caretaker said,
When I was a boy.

The children studied each relic as it came down,
But made no notes.
They said, we're taking that mossed-up one
For the Nature Table.

The caretaker cleared the guttering.
He put his ladder away.
And the children kicked the least un-bouncy ball
In the empty playground.

The Mysteries of Zigomar

I'd like to tell you what they are
The Mysteries of Zigomar.

I think it's time to spill the beans
And spell out what the whole thing means.

Remove the mask, reveal the trail
Unbag the cat and lift the veil.

Yes, lay my cards upon the table
And see an end to myth and fable.

Say, Here it is! and, There we are!
The Mysteries of Zigomar.

No more delay, no dark confusion
Just simple facts and a conclusion.

I think it's time, I think it's late
The world has had too long to wait.

From Stoke-on-Trent to Cooch Behar
We're driven mad by Zigomar.

From long ago to times like these
One tangled web of mysteries.

But not much longer – Goodbye doubt!
The time has come to spit it out.

I'd like to tell you what they are
The Mysteries of Zigomar.

I'd like to tell, you'd *love* to hear . . .
The trouble is, I've no idea.

Only Snow

Outside, the sky was almost brown.
The clouds were hanging low.
Then all of a sudden it happened:
The air was full of snow.

The children rushed to the windows.
The teacher let them go,
Though she teased them for their foolishness.
After all, it was only snow.

It was only snow that was falling,
Only out of the sky,
Only on to the turning earth
Before the blink of an eye.

What else could it do from up there,
But fall in the usual way?
It was only *weather*, really.
What else could you say?

The teacher sat at her desk
Putting ticks in a little row,
While the children stared through steamy glass
At the only snow.

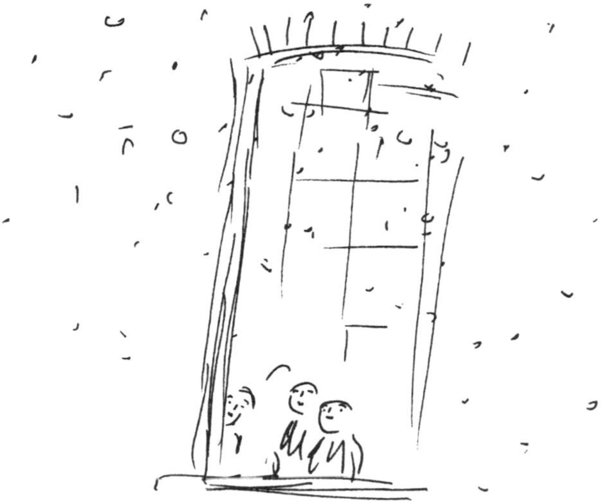

5
The Vampire and the Hound

The Secrets of the Staffroom

You may well think y'knows it all,
You cheeky kids today,
But I 'ave got a tale to tell
To blow y'minds away;
About your teachers, cruel and kind,
Quick-witted, vile and slow,
And the secrets of the staffroom if . . .
Y'really want to know.

Y'may suppose they sits in there
Just drinking pots of tea,
With nice triangular sandwiches
Politely as can be.
Well, that was maybe how it was
Back then, but not today.
More like it's now a crate of beer
And a Chinese take-away.

Y'might have guessed the place was full
Of markin', books and chalk;
Educational supplements
And intellectual talk.
The plays of William Shakespeare,
The exports of Brazil,
But never a pile of bettin' slips
From that well-known William 'ill.

Perhaps y'thought they spend their time
With felt pens, paint and glue,
Worrying themselves to death
To do their best for you.
While some, it's true, are softies,
There's others 'ard as sin,
A-jabbin' Playdoh infants with
A nasty little pin.

There's teachers, every school has some,
Who work until they drop,
To help their lucky pupils climb
The ladder to the top.
There's others, though, with bloodshot eyes
Below a crafty frown,
Who sharpen up the staffroom axe
To chop the ladder down.

I knew a staffroom once that 'ad
A trap door in the floor,
That led down to an . . . awful place,
I'd rather not say more.
When governors came calling,
It always was the rule,
They never found a single
Trouble-maker in that school.

You may have wondered how I know
These things of which I speak.
Well, I was once a caretaker
For ninety quid a week.
But since I've gone and blown the gaff
And give the game away,
The staffroom mob is on my trail
And it's *me* who'll 'ave to pay.

So watch y'steps and peel y'eyes
And keep y'noses clean;
The secrets of the staffroom ain't
For all – see what I mean?
Beyond that door there lies a place
You never oughter go.
Unless, of course, you're curious and . . .
Y'really want to know.

The Grey Boys

Oh Mother may I go to play
With the grey boys in the street
For I hear the thud of a booted ball
And the clattering of feet.

My window overlooks the street
The street lamps light the game
The boys are mad to kick the ball
And I feel just the same.

A yellow haze hangs round the lamps
Under the smoky sky
And up and down the clattery street
The shadowy boys go by.

Oh Mother may I join the game
With the grey boys of the town
For I feel much better than I did
And my temperature is down.

My fevered brow is cooler now
My pulse is calm and slow
My hands lie still upon the quilt
Oh Mother . . . may I go?

Dream Football

Dream football is the harder game
The grass is devilishly long
And growing
Fish appear in the trainer's bucket
Your mother has set up a small shop
On the halfway line
You are obliged to play in your underpants.

The Mad Professor's Daughter

She came into the classroom
In a dress as black as night
And her eyes were green as grass
And her face was paper-white.
She was tall and quite unsmiling,
Though her manner was polite.

Yes, her manner was polite
As she stood with Mrs Porter
And you never would have guessed
She was the Mad Professor's daughter.

'A new girl,' said the teacher.
'Her name is Margaret Bell.
She's just arrived this morning.
She's not been very well.'
And we stared into those grass-green eyes
And sank beneath their spell.

Yes, we sank beneath their spell
Like swimmers under water
And found ourselves in thrall
To the Mad Professor's daughter.

The sky outside was overcast;
Rain hung in the air
And splattered on the window panes
As we sat waiting there.
Our fate, we knew, was settled,
Yet we hardly seemed to care.

Yes, we hardly seemed to care,
As the clock ticked past the quarter,
That we had lost our lives
To the Mad Professor's daughter.

We did our sums in a sort of trance,
'Played' at half-past ten,
Sang songs in the hall for half an hour,
Ate lunch and played again.
And all the while, like a constant ache,
We wondered 'Where?' and 'When?'

Yes, where and when and how and why,
And what ill luck had brought her?
And whether we might yet deny
The Mad Professor's daughter.

She made no move at two o'clock.
She made no move at three.
A wisp of hope rose in our hearts
And thoughts of 'mum' and 'tea'.
And then she spoke the fatal words,
Just four: 'Come home with me!'

She spoke the words 'Come home with me'
The way her father taught her;
Her green eyes fixed unblinkingly,
The Mad Professor's daughter.

And now an extra sense of dread
Seeped into every soul;
The hamster cowered in its cage,
The fish flinched in its bowl.
We put our chairs up on the desks
And heard the thunder roll.

Yes, we heard the thunder roll
As we turned from Mrs Porter
And set off through the town
With the Mad Professor's daughter.

Her silent lips were red as blood.
Her step was firm (alas!)
And the people on the street
Stood aside to let us pass.
Though this piper played no tune,
She had enthralled a whole class.

A whole class, like sheep we were,
Like lambs to the slaughter,
With PE bags and such
Behind the Mad Professor's daughter.

The rain beat down upon our heads.
The wind was warm and wild.
Wet trees blew all around us,
As up a drive we filed.
Then a mad face at a window
Stared out at us – and smiled.

Yes, a mad face at a window
That streamed with running water,
While lightning lit the sky above
The Mad Professor's daughter.

And now the end has almost come;
We wait here in despair
With chains upon our arms and legs
And cobwebs in our hair.
And hear her voice outside the door,
His foot upon the stair.

Yes, his foot upon the stair:
'Oh, save us, Mrs Porter!'
Don't leave us to the father of
The Mad Professor's daughter.

*

A final word – a warning:
Please heed this tale I tell.
If you should meet a quiet girl
Whose name is Margaret Bell,
Don't look into her grass-green eyes
Or you'll be lost as well.

Yes, you'd be lost as well,
However hard you fought her,
And curse until the day you died
The Mad Professor's daughter.

Cemetery Road

When I was a boy
Just nine years old,
We moved to a house
On Cemetery Road.

The road was rough
Not well-to-do.
It split
The cemetery in two.

On winter nights
The gravestones glowed
In streetlamp shine
On Cemetery Road.

When coming home
My heart would beat
From footsteps
That were not my feet.

On frosty evenings
Scared to death
By breathing
That was not my breath.

Until at times
I'd quite explode
And run for my life
Down Cemetery Road.

Along the entry,
Velvet black,
Into the house
And not look back.

Yet now, alas,
My pulse has slowed.
I'm quite grown up.
It's just a road.

The Vampire and the Hound

Towards the distant mountains flying,
Closer, closer,
In darkness, wind and rain;
Above the ancient castle sighing,
Nearer, nearer,
The Vampire comes again.

In at my Lady's window staring,
Closer, closer,
His pale eyes calm and dead,
Watching the beeswax candle flaring,
Nearer, nearer,
Beside my Lady's bed.

Over the golden carpet going,
Closer, closer,
His black cloak furled and wet,
Up to the bed where, all unknowing,
Nearer, nearer,
My Lady's sleeping yet.

Come at last to his monstrous calling,
Closer, closer,
Unchecked by keep or moat,
The Vampire, swooning low and falling,
Nearer, nearer,
Towards my Lady's throat.

Wakes to a nightmare foul, and screaming,
Murder, murder!
My Lady, silken-gowned.
Up from the hearth-rug, damply steaming,
Save her, save her!
Lottie, my Lady's Hound.

Black night and rain at the windows lashing,
Louder, louder,
Warm blood upon the floor,
Blood on the silken sheets a-splashing,
Redder, redder,
Blows on the bolted door.

The savaged Vampire, faint and fleeing,
Horror, horror!
The sundered door gapes wide.
Servants aghast at the sight they're seeing;
Save us, save us!
The Hound with a bleeding side.

My Lady there at the bedside kneeling,
Weeping, weeping,
Stroking her saviour's head.
Fire-thrown shapes on the distant ceiling,
Higher, higher,
And Lottie, the brave dog . . . dead.

6
How to Score Goals

The Lovely Ball of Leather

About a mile North of Preston
On a cool November day
A team of boys plus substitutes
Was setting off to play.
They sat there in the minibus
Just gazing straight ahead
Listening to their manager
And this is what he said.

O boys, he cried, O fellas
I couldn't ask for more
You run your little socks off
Though you never seem to score.
But I know you'll keep on trying
You'll strive and strain and sweat
Till that lovely ball of leather
Goes flying in the net.

Just a little West of Bromwich
In the January rain
That selfsame team of players
Was on the road again.
They crowded in the minibus
As it carried them away
While their manager-cum-driver
Had these quiet words to say.

O boys, he cried, O fellas
I've got this rotten cold
My knee's a bit arthritic
And I'm really rather old.
But I know I will recover
My life's not over yet
Till that lovely ball of leather
Goes flying in the net.

In a lay-by South of Hampton
On a balmy April night
When the road was dark and empty
And the sky was starry bright,
A team of boys plus substitutes
Was sitting in the bus
Eating chips and burgers
While their manager spoke thus.

O boys, he cried, O fellas
I *knew* that you could play
I knew the gods were with us
And we'd get a goal some day.
It was a precious moment
Which I never will forget
When that lovely ball of leather
Went flying in the net.

Team Talk

Marcus, don't argue with the ref.
Yes, he needs glasses
Yes, he should keep up with the play
Yes, yes, he's a pawn
In some international betting syndicate
But *don't argue with him.*
He'll send you off.
And if he doesn't, I will.

Billy, you're the goalie – right?
Listen, you're *allowed* to use your hands
OK?
It's in the rules
It's legal.

Another thing
What's that you've got in the back of the net?
That carrier bag
I've seen it – what is it?
Hm.
Well, leave-it-a-lone
You can eat later.

Now then, Michael
You've got Charles outside you, OK?
Unmarked, OK?
I know he's only your brother
But pass to him.

Marcus, another thing
Don't argue with the linesman either
Or me, for that matter
Or *anybody*
Just —
Just —
Just —
Marcus . . . shut up.

Kevin, a word.
Their number seven
You're supposed to be marking him
And he's scored five already, right?
Well that's . . . enough
Close him down.

So come on, lads
The golden rules – remember?
Hold your positions
Run into space
Call for the ball
Play to the whistle
Pass only to members of your own team.

Last of all
NEVER GIVE UP
Thirteen–nil
Sounds bad, but it's not the end.
We can turn it round
We can get a result
It's a game of two halves.

So let's go out there –
And show 'em!

Billy . . . are you eating?

Team Talk 2
(the next match)

Marcus, what did I say?
I warned you
You're *argumentative*
He was bound to send you off
Your own mother would send you off.
And besides –
Besides –
Besides –
Marcus . . . shut up.

Dominic, a word.
Mud.
Stop worrying about it, OK?
There's no prize for the cleanest pair of shorts
Never mind what your auntie says
Get stuck in.

No, Jonathan, that old fella on the line
Is *not* a scout for Man. United.
No.
No, he isn't.
Don't ask me how I know
I just do.
Call it instinct.

Come here, you two
Michael – this is Charles
Charles – this is Michael
Say, Hallo.
Say, Pleased to meet you.
I *mean* it.
Now *pass* to each other.

Billy, empty your pockets
All of 'em.
What's this?
Goalkeeping's an art, Billy
It's vital
The last line of defence
You have to *concentrate*
And how can you expect to do that
With a pocketful of peanuts?
Get rid of 'em.

How many shirts are you wearing,
Craig – hm?
It's not that cold
You look like . . .
No, not *me*, Marcus
You look like – well, never mind.

Brian, brilliant header.
Unstoppable.
Now let's see if you can do it again
At their end.

Yes, and another thing
I know your dad's an expert
I can hear him
We can all hear him
But take no notice – right?
If I'd wanted you to play through the middle
I would not have picked you
At left back.

So let's get out there
Keep plugging away
They're not eight goals better than us
Anyway ten men are sometimes harder to beat
Than a full team. Right?

And remember *Golden Rules*
NEVER-GIVE-UP.

Billy . . . is that a biscuit?
Mmm. Just what I need.

Team Talk 14

Lads, believe me
You know it
I know it
We are not the best team
In this league
But this lot –
Marcus, are you listening?
This lot
I have to say it –
Are worse!

Believe me
We can beat 'em
What am I saying –
We *are* beating 'em!
Yippee!

So this is the situation, lads
Stay calm
Stay focused
Get out there –
Yes, *now* Billy –

Get out there
And whatever it was you were doing –
This is the plan, right Michael?
Right Charles?
Whatever it *was* you were *doing*
Keep doing it.

OK?

Dad on the Line
(or a boy's nightmare)

I'm playing in this big game
New kit, great pitch
Proper goals with proper nets.

All of a sudden
With rattle and scarf
And a flask of tea . . . there's Dad.

Come on, my son! says Dad
Square ball! says Dad
We are the champions! says Dad
Que sera, sera.

*

I'm playing now in a bigger game
Brand-new ball, managers in dugouts
Proper linesmen and a proper ref.

All of a sudden
With our dog on a lead
And a meat pie . . . there's Dad.

Come on you reds! says Dad
Up the Rovers! says Dad
We're going to Wem-b-ley! says Dad
Que sera, sera.

*

And now the biggest game of all
Changing rooms with sunken baths
Proper turnstiles and a proper stand.

All of a sudden
With his mates from work
And a giant photograph of me . . . there's Dad.

Offside! says Dad
Foul! says Dad
That's my lad out there! says Dad
Que sera, sera.

Then, usually at this point
He runs onto the pitch.
The stewards chase him
(He's still got the giant photo)
The crowd goes mad
The ref stares accusingly at me . . .

And I wake up.

How to Score Goals

(1)
Approach with ball
Point left
Say, 'Ooh, look – a bunny rabbit!'
Shoot right
Goal.

(2)
Approach with ball
Point right
Say, 'Ooh, look – a fiver!'
Shoot left
Goal.

(3)
Approach with ball
Say, 'Sorry about all this trickery
I never saw any rabbit'
Offer to shake hands
Shoot.

(4)
Approach with ball
Sudden sound of bagpipes
(For this you will need an accomplice)
Goal.

(5)
Approach with ball
Plus cake
Sing 'Happy Birthday to you!'
Invite goalie
To blow his candles out
etc.

(6)
Approach with ball
Point skywards
Say, 'Ooh, look – a vulture!'
(He will have forgotten the rabbit by this time)
Goal.

(7)
Approach with ball
Say, 'I bet I can hit you with this next shot'
Shoot.

(8)
Approach with ball
Say, 'I am being sponsored for charity
A pound for every goal I score'
Shoot
Shoot
Shoot.

(9)
Approach with ball
Say, 'Smart boots you've got there
Very smart
Not like these old things of mine
Still, Dad'll get a job soon
Then
When Mum comes out of hospital
And the baby's had his —'
Shoot.

(10)
Approach with ball
Sudden eclipse of sun
(For this you will need to consult astronomical charts)
Goal.

(11)
Approach with ball
Think of something . . .
Goal.

Talk Us Through It, Charlotte

Well I shouldn't've been playin' really
Only there to watch me brother.
My friend fancies his friend, y'know.
Anyway they was a man short.

Stay out on the wing, they said
Give 'em something to think about.
So I did that for about an hour;
Never passed to me or anything.

The ball kind of rebounded to me.
I thought, I'll have a little run with it.
I mean, they wasn't passin' to me
Was they? So off I went.

I ran past this first boy
He sort of fell over.
It was a bit slippery on that grass
I will say that for him.

Two more of 'em come at me
Only they sort of tackled each other
Collided – arh.* I kept going.
There was this great big fat boy.

* Rhymes with 'car' – Charlotte's a Black Country girl.

167

One way or another I kicked it
Through his legs and run round him.
That took a time. Me brother
Was shouting, Pass it to me, like.

Well like I said, I'd been there an hour.
They never give *me* a pass
Never even spoke to me
Or anything. So I kept going.

Beat this other boy somehow
Then there was just the goalie.
Out he came, spreadin' himself
As they say. I was really worried.

I thought he was going to hug me.
So I dipped me shoulder like they do
And the goalie moved one way, y'know
And I slammed it in the net.

Turned out afterwards it was the winner.
The manager said I was very good.
He wants me down at trainin' on Tuesday.
My friend says she's comin' as well.

Surely This Boy
Must Play for England

In an ordinary house in an ordinary room
In an ordinary single bed
An ordinary boy in pyjamas
Flicks a casual goal with his head.

Surely this boy must play for England.

Helps his dad after breakfast
To wash and polish the car
Beats his man in the garage
And hammers one in off the bar.

It's madness – he's only ten.

Helps his mum in the afternoon
With the supermarket trip
While clearing a wall of shoppers
With a David Beckham chip.

If he's good enough, he's old enough.

Plays with his little sister
Takes the dog for a stroll
And dumbfounds the local pigeons
With an unbelievable goal.

Ten-year-old makes the squad.

Eats his tea in the evening
Talks to his gran on the phone
Faces four giant defenders
And takes them on on his own.

Surely this boy *must* play for England.

Cleans his teeth in the bathroom
Draws in the steamy glass
Shuffles his feet on the bathroom mat
And flicks a casual pass.

Youngest-ever sub takes the field.

In an ordinary house in an ordinary room
In an ordinary single bed
An ordinary boy plays for England
And stands the game on its head.

A hat-trick, and he's still only ten.

Leaves the ground with the match ball
While his mother tidies the pitch
And his dad turns off the floodlights
With a casual flick of the switch.

They think it's all over.

Just an ordinary boy in pyjamas
Fast asleep at the end of the day
Though his feet still twitch in the darkness
And he's never too tired . . . to play.

Soccer Sonnet

Now children, said the teacher with a smile
Put down your books and let your pencils fall
Come out into the playground for a while
And run around with me and kick a ball.
We'll pick two teams and use our coats for goals
(But leave our bags and worries at the door)
And play the game with all our hearts and souls
And never mind the weather or the score.
I'll promise not to test your soccer skills
The ball's the only thing you'll need to pass
There'll be no Key Stage Three or spelling drills
There'll be no top or bottom of the class.
So let's forget the gold stars for a day
And get outside – and run around – and play.

1966, or Were You There, Daddy?

In the fabulous year of '66
The year beyond compare
When England carried off the cup
Dear Daddy, were you there?

Yes, my son, I was there.

When Bobby Charlton ran midfield
And Hurst leapt in the air
And Peters drifted down the wing
Dear Daddy, were you there?

Yes, my son, absolutely.

When Nobby Stiles snapped at their heels
And Wilson played it square
And Gordon Banks was flying
Dear Daddy, were you there?

Yes, my son, no question.

When Bobby Moore was in control
And Ball was everywhere
And Beckenbauer was trouble
Dear Daddy, were you there?

Yes, my son, I really was.

When England carried off the cup
And anthems filled the air
And Wembley was the place to be
Dear Daddy, were *you* there?

Oh yes, my son, oh yes, oh yes
Oh yes I was *really* there.
When Bobby Charlton ran midfield
And Peters played it square
And big Jack Charlton headed out
And Hunt was everywhere
And Cohen tackled like a tank
And Beckenbauer showed flair
And Gordon Banks was flying . . .
           flying
Your dad, Oh-he-was-there!

The Betsy Street Booters

We are the Betsy Street Booters
We are the girls you can't beat
The sharpest and straightest of shooters
On twenty-two talented feet.

The boys in our school think we're clueless
Which just shows how little they know
We played them last week in the playground
And beat them five times in a row.

The boys say our tactics are rubbish
Soccer skills nought out of ten
We played them once more on a real pitch
And beat them all over again.

The boys in our school blame the weather
The bounce and a bad referee
We played them in glorious sunshine
And hammered them 17–3.

The boys now appear quite disheartened
And wonder just what they should do
They're talking of taking up netball . . .
But we're pretty good at that too.

We are the Betsy Street Booters
We are the girls you can't beat
The sharpest and straightest of shooters
On twenty-two talented feet.

Who Kicked Cock Robin?

Not I said the owl
Gazing down sleepy-eyed
I'm not that kind of fowl
And we're on the same side.

Not I said the bee
Buzzing back to his hive
Cock Robin kicked me
And then took a dive.

Not I said the grub
My excuse is complete
I was only a sub
And – I ain't got no feet.

The Song of the Sub

I'm standing on the touchline
In my substitute's kit
As though it doesn't matter
And I don't mind a bit.

I'm trying to be patient
Trying not to hope
That my friends play badly
And the team can't cope.

I'm a sub, I'm a sub and I sing this song
And I'm only ever wanted when things go wrong.

When a boy has the measles
When a boy goes lame
The teacher turns to me
And I get a game.

When a boy gets kicked
Or shows up late
And they need another player
I'm the candidate.

I'm a sub, I'm a sub and I sing this song
And I'm only ever wanted when things go wrong.

I warm up on the touchline
I stretch and bend
And wonder what disasters
My luck will send.

If a boy got lost
Or ran away to France
If a boy got *kidnapped*
Would I get my chance?

I'm a sub, I'm a sub and I sing this song
And I'm only ever wanted when things go wrong.

I feel a bit embarrassed
That I'm not bothered more
When decisions go against us
And the other teams score.

I try to keep my spirits up
I juggle with the ball
And hope to catch the teacher's eye
It does no good at all.

Just a sub, just a sub till my dying day
And I only get a kick when the others can't play.

I'm standing on the touchline
On the very same spot
And it *does* really matter
And I *do* mind – a lot.

I think I'll hang my boots up
It's not the game for me
Then suddenly I hear those words:
You're on! I am? *Yippee!*

Friendly Matches

In friendly matches
Players exchange pleasantries
Hallo, George!
How's the Missus?
Admire opponents' kit
Smart shirt, Bert!
Sympathize with linesmen
Difficult decision, there.
And share their half-time oranges.

In friendly matches
Players apologize for heavy tackles
How clumsy of me.
And offer assistance with throw-ins
Allow us to help you with that heavy ball.

In friendly matches
Players and substitutes alike
Speak well of referees
First-rate official
Sound knowledge of the game
Excellent eyesight!

In friendly matches
Players celebrate opposing players' birthdays
With corner-flag candles
On pitch-shaped cakes.

In friendly matches
Players take it in turns
No, no, please, after *you*

to score.

Kicking a Ball

What I like best
Yes, most of all
In my whole life
Is kicking a ball.
Kicking a ball
Kicking a ball
Not songs on the bus
Or hymns in the hall
Not running or rounders
But kicking a ball.

Not eating an ice-cream
Or riding a bike
No – kicking a ball
Is what I like.
Not baking a cake
Or swimming the crawl
Not painting a picture
Or knitting a shawl
Not reading a book
Or writing a letter
No – kicking a ball
Is twenty times better!

Yes, kicking a ball
Kicking a ball
With Clive and Trevor
Malcolm and Paul
Or even without them
Just me and a wall.
My legs might be skinny
My feet might be small
But I get a kick
Out of kicking a ball.

Not punching a ball
Or bashing a ball
Serving a ball
Or smashing a ball
Not throwing a ball
Or blowing a ball
Not bowling or batting
Or patting a ball
Not pinging or ponging
Or potting or putting
But booting and shooting
Yes, kicking, oh, kicking!
Just kicking a ball.

A ball in the playground
A ball on the grass
A shot on the run
A dribble, a pass
A ball before breakfast
A ball before bed
A dream of a ball
A 'kick' in the head.

Don't want a ball
That's odd or screw
That you hit with a mallet
Or a billiard cue.
Don't want a ball
That's made of meat
I'd really rather
Score than eat!
Mothballs crumble
Snowballs melt
Give me a ball
You can save – and belt!

Not a ball-cock
Or a ball-point
Or a plastic ball-
And-socket joint.
Not a ball-bearing
(Bit too small)
But – putting it more or less
Baldly – a ball.

Kicking a ball
Kicking a ball
That's surely the purpose
Of life, after all.
Not climbing a mountain
In far Nepal
Or diving for pearls
In the Bay of Bengal.
Not sailing a yacht
On a tight haul
In a sudden squall
To Montreal.
But kicking a ball
Kicking a ball
Kick, kick, kick, kick,
Kicking a ball!

And later on
As the years pass
I'll still be running
Across the grass
Kicking a ball
Kicking a ball
With Clive and Malcolm
Trevor and Paul.
Not reading the paper
Or having a shave
But forcing the goalie
To make a save.
Not kissing the wife
Or bathing the baby
But kicking a ball
And scoring! (maybe)
Till baby toddles
And *tackles* and then . . .
Starts the ball rolling
All over again.

Yes, life's a circle
Endless and small
And when all's said and done
The world's a ball.

What I like best
Yes, most of all
In my whole life
Is kicking a ball.
In freezing cold
Or blinding heat
Ever and always
A ball at my feet.
Caked in mud
Covered in sweat
Scoring the goals
I'll never forget.
With Paul and Malcolm
Trevor and Clive
Completely exhausted
And *really* alive . . .

And kicking, yes, kicking
Oh, kicking!
Wow! Kicking a ball.

7
Scissors

Teachers' Prayer

Let the children in our care
Clean their shoes and comb their hair;
Come to school on time – and neat,
Blow their noses, wipe their feet.
Let them, Lord, *not* eat in class
Or rush into the hall *en masse*.
Let them show some self-control;
Let them slow down; let them *stroll*.

Let the children in our charge
Not be violent or large;
Not be sick on the school-trip bus,
Not be cleverer than us;
Not be unwashed, loud or mad,
(With a six-foot mother or a seven-foot dad).
Let them, please, say 'drew' not 'drawed';
Let them *know the answers*, Lord.

Slow Reader

I – am – in – the – slow
read – ers – group – my – broth
er – is – in – the – foot
ball – team – my – sis – ter
is – a – ser – ver – my
lit – tle – broth – er – was
a – wise – man – in – the
in – fants – christ – mas – play
I – am – in – the – slow
read – ers – group – that – is
all – I – am – in – I
hate – it.

There's a Fish Tank

There's a fish tank
In our class
With no fish in it;
A guinea-pig cage
With no guinea-pig in it;
A formicarium
With no ants in it;
And according to Miss Hodge
Some of our heads
Are empty too.

There's a stock-cupboard
With no stock,
Flowerpots without flowers,
Plimsolls without owners
And me without a friend
For a week
While he goes on holiday.

There's a girl
With no front teeth,
And a boy with hardly any hair
Having had it cut.
There are sums without answers,
Paintings unfinished
And projects with no hope
Of ever coming to an end.
According to Miss Hodge
The only thing that's brim-full
In our class
Is the waste-paper basket.

Glenis

The teacher says:

Why is it, Glenis,
Please answer me this,
The only time
You ever stop talking in class
Is if I ask you
Where's the Khyber Pass?
Or when was the Battle of Waterloo?
Or what is nine times three?
Or how do you spell
Mississippi?
Why is it, Glenis,
The only time you are silent
Is when I ask you a question?

And Glenis says:

Mr Bloor

There was a man named Mr Bloor
Who liked to referee *and* score.

He'd blow his whistle, swing his boot
Beat half a dozen boys – and shoot.

(He was a teacher in our school
His favourite team was Liverpool.)

He also loved to commentate
'Bloor's got the ball – Bloor's going great!

He's beat his man, what rare control
He's round the full back now and – GOAL!

His legs are strong, his brain is quick!'
(Sometimes he'd let *us* have a kick.)

But Mr Bloor the referee
Was also fair, as you will see.

He'd score a goal and strut with pride
Then stop and rule himself offside.

He'd cover back and tackle hard
Yet give himself a yellow card,

Bulldoze boys caught in his path
And send himself for an early bath.

On rare occasions I recall
Our Mr Bloor would *pass* the ball,

Leaving some kid, like Vinny Cole
(Who never scored), with an open goal.

'It's Vinny now, all full of dinner
Dazzling footwork and – the winner!'

Mr Bloor was short and wide
He played with trousers tucked inside

His ordinary socks and on his head
He wore a bobble hat, bright red.

Sometimes his girlfriend, Miss Levine
(She taught us too), would run the line.

She'd stand there smiling, tall and slim
And wave her little flag at him.

Eventually his knees gave way
And doctors said he shouldn't play.

Now Mr Bloor's a mere spectator
Oh yes of course *and* commentator.

'He's got the ball, what sweet control
Deceives the goalie now and – GOAL!'

Colin

When you frown at me like that, Colin,
And wave your arm in the air,
I know just what you're going to say:
'Please, Sir, it isn't fair!'

It isn't fair
On the football field
If their team scores a goal.
It isn't fair
In a cricket match.
Unless you bat *and* bowl.

When you scowl at me that way, Colin,
And mutter and slam your chair,
I always know what's coming next:
'Please, Sir, it isn't fair!'

It isn't fair
When I give you a job.
It isn't fair when I don't.
If I keep you in
It isn't fair.
If you're told to go out, you won't.

When heads bow low in assembly
And the whole school's saying a prayer,
I can guess what's on your mind, Colin:
'Our Father . . . it isn't fair!'

It wasn't fair
In the Infants.
It isn't fair now.
It won't be fair
At the Comprehensive
(For first years, anyhow).

When your life reaches its end, Colin,
Though I doubt if I'll be there,
I can picture the words on the gravestone now.
They'll say: IT IS NOT FAIR.

The Cane

The teacher
had some thin springy sticks
for making kites.

Reminds me
of the old days, he said;
and swished one.

The children
near his desk laughed nervously,
and pushed closer.

A cheeky girl
held out her cheeky hand.
Go on, Sir!

said her friends.
Give her the stick, she's always
playing up!

The teacher
paused, then did as he was told.
Just a tap.

Oh, Sir!
We're going to tell on you,
the children said.

Other children
left their seats and crowded round
the teacher's desk.

Other hands
went out. Making kites was soon
forgotten.

My turn next!
He's had one go already!
That's not fair!

Soon the teacher,
to save himself from the crush,
called a halt.

(It was
either that or use the cane
for real.)

Reluctantly,
the children did as they were told
and sat down.

If you behave
yourselves, the teacher said,
I'll cane you later.

Scissors

Nobody leave the room.
Everyone listen to me.
We had ten pairs of scissors
At half-past two,
And now there's only three.

Seven pairs of scissors
Disappeared from sight.
Not one of you leaves
Till we find them.
We can stop here all night!

Scissors don't lose themselves,
Melt away or explode.
Scissors have not got
Legs of their own
To go running off up the road.

We really need those scissors,
That's what makes me mad.
If it was seven pairs
Of children we'd lost,
It wouldn't be so bad.

I don't want to hear excuses.
Don't anyone speak.
Just ransack this room
Till we find them,
Or we'll stop here . . . all week!

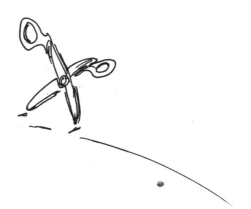

Complaint

The teachers all sit in the staffroom.
The teachers all drink tea.
The teachers all smoke cigarettes
As cosy as can be.

We have to go out at playtime
Unless we bring a note
Or it's tipping down with rain
Or we haven't got a coat.

We have to go out at playtime
Whether we like it or not.
And freeze to death if it's freezing
And boil to death if it's hot.

The teachers can sit in the staffroom
And have a cosy chat.
We have to go out at playtime;
Where's the fairness in that?

Picking Teams

When we pick teams in the playground,
Whatever the game might be,
There's always somebody left till last
And usually it's me.

I stand there looking hopeful
And tapping myself on the chest,
But the captains pick the others first,
Starting, of course, with the best.

Maybe if teams were sometimes picked
Starting with the worst,
Once in his life a boy like me
Could end up being first!

reading test

tree	little	milk	egg	book
read	ing	test	I	took
school	sit	frog	playing	bun
it	was	not	much	fun
flower	road	clock	train	light
still	I	got	it	right
picture	think	summer	peo . . .	
			popple . . .	
			peep . . .	
			pe . . .	
			p . . . well, nearly.	

The Runners

We're hopeless at racing,
Me and my friend.
I'm slow at the start,
She's slow at the end.

She has the stitch,
I get sore feet,
And neither one of us
Cares to compete.

But co-operation's
A different case.
You should see us
In the three-legged race!

Parents' Evening

We're waiting in the corridor,
My dad, my mum and me.
They're sitting there and talking;
I'm nervous as can be.
I wonder what she'll tell 'em.
I'll say I've got a pain!
I wish I'd got my spellings right.
I wish I had a brain.

We're waiting in the corridor,
My husband, son and me.
My son just stands there smiling;
I'm smiling, nervously.
I wonder what she'll tell us.
I hope it's not *all* bad.
He's such a good boy, really;
But dozy – like his dad.

We're waiting in the corridor,
My wife, my boy and me.
My wife's as cool as cucumber;
I'm nervous as can be.
I hate these parents' evenings.
The waiting makes me sick.
I feel just like a kid again
Who's gonna get the stick.

I'm waiting in the classroom.
It's nearly time to start.
I wish there was a way to stop
The pounding in my heart.
The parents in the corridor
Are chatting cheerfully;
And now I've got to face them,
And I'm nervous as can be.

Back to School

In the last week of the holidays
I was feeling glum.
I could hardly wait for school to start;
Neither could Mum.

Now we've been back a week,
I could do with a breather.
I can hardly wait for the holidays;
Teacher can't either.

Supply Teacher

Here is the rule for what to do
Whenever your teacher has the flu,
Or for some other reason takes to her bed
And a different teacher comes instead.

When this visiting teacher hangs up her hat,
Writes the date on the board, does this or that,
Always remember, you must say this:
'Our teacher never does that, Miss!'

When you want to change places or wander about,
Or feel like getting the guinea-pig out,
Never forget, the message is this:
'Our teacher always lets us, Miss!'

Then, when your teacher returns next day
And complains about the paint or clay,
Remember these words, you just say this:
'That *other* teacher told us to, Miss!'

Headmaster's Hymn
(to be sung)

When a knight won his spurs
In the stories of old,
He was – 'Face the front, David Briggs,
What have you been told?'
With a shield on his arm
And a lance in his – 'Hey!
Is that a ball I can see?
Put – it – a – way.'

No charger have I
And – 'No talking back there.
You're supposed to be singing,
Not combing your hair.'
Though back into storyland
Giants have – 'Roy,
This isn't the playground,
Stop pushing that boy!'

Let faith be my shield
And – 'Who's eating sweets here?
I'm ashamed of you, Marion,
It's not like you, dear.'
And let me set free
With – 'Please stop that, Paul King.
This is no place for whistlers,
We'd rather you sing!'

The School Nurse

We're lining up to see the nurse
And in my opinion there's nothing worse.
It is the thing I always dread.
Supposing I've got *nits* in my head.

I go inside and sit on the chair.
She ruffles her fingers in my hair.
I feel my face getting hot and red.
Supposing she finds *nits* in my head.

It's taking ages; it must be bad.
Oh, how shall I tell my mum and dad?
I'd rather see the dentist instead
Than be the one with *nits* in his head.

Then she taps my arm and says, 'Next please!'
And I'm out in the corridor's cooling breeze.
Yet still I can feel that sense of dread.
Supposing she *had* found nits in my head.

Please Mrs Butler

Please Mrs Butler
This boy Derek Drew
Keeps copying my work, Miss.
What shall I do?

Go and sit in the hall, dear.
Go and sit in the sink.
Take your books on the roof, my lamb.
Do whatever you think.

Please Mrs Butler
This boy Derek Drew
Keeps taking my rubber, Miss.
What shall I do?

Keep it in your hand, dear.
Hide it up your vest.
Swallow it if you like, my love.
Do what you think best.

Please Mrs Butler
This boy Derek Drew
Keeps calling me rude names, Miss.
What shall I do?

Lock yourself in the cupboard, dear.
Run away to sea.
Do whatever you can, my flower.
But *don't ask me*.

8
Dog in
the Playground

The Ordeal of Robin Hood

There is a new boy in our class;
He came the other day.
He hadn't any friends, of course,
So we let him be in our play.

That was the first mistake we made.

The play was called 'Bold Robin Hood';
We'd practised it all week.
The new boy missed rehearsals
So he had no lines to speak.

He thought of a few, though, as you will see.

Besides, this boy was foreign,
His English wasn't good.
He said his name was Janek;
He'd not heard of Robin Hood.

Robin Hood didn't get to Poland, Miss Hodge said.

Well, first we pushed the desks back
To make a bigger space.
Then we hung this curtain up
For the outlaws' hiding place.

Miss Hodge just let us get on with it.

Kevin Jukes was Robin Hood,
Roy was Little John,
I was the Sheriff of Nottingham –
I had this red cloak on.

The new boy was one of my guards, supposedly.

The swords we had were rulers;
The cupboard, Robin's den;
And most of us had moustaches
Drawn with black felt pen.

Roy's was navy blue, but you could hardly tell.

The rest of the class sat round to watch,
Miss Hodge was watching too.
Then Keith announced the title
And who was playing who.

Keith was also Friar Tuck with a cushion
up his coat.

At first it all went pretty well,
Mistakes we made were slight;
The trouble only started
When we got to the first fight.

There should have been three fights altogether;
should have been.

What we'd practised was an ambush
To rescue Friar Tuck,
With me and my guards just riding by
Until the outlaws struck.

No horses, of course, just 'clip-clop' noises.

So there was I, my cloak tossed back,
Duelling with Robin Hood;
While Janek – I didn't know it then –
Was guarding me more than he should.

Perhaps there's nothing in the Polish language
for 'Aaargh!'

Guards, you see, are meant to fight
For a little while, then lose.
Get captured, killed or wounded,
Whatever way they choose.

Usually our plays had guns in them, only this
time Miss Hodge said she was sick of guns.

But Janek wasn't having that,
He wouldn't even defend;
And the way he was generally carrying on,
The play would never end.

That was the second mistake we made: it ended
all right.

And still the worst was yet to come
In Robin Hood's ordeal:
Not only wouldn't Janek die,
He was sword-fighting for real!

The Merrie Men were looking less merry by the
minute.

Will Scarlett's hand was stinging
From the blows that Janek smote,
And Friar Tuck was thankful
For that cushion up his coat.

Alan-a-Dale and Little John were already
behind the curtain.

We did our best to stop him;
Tried 'whispering' in his ear;
But he was shouting foreign words,
We couldn't make him hear.

*I could see then how Poland knocked us out of
the World Cup.*

The play was going haywire now,
The audience could tell.
When some of the guards tried changing sides,
Janek polished them off as well.

*'Pole-ished' – get it? Keith thought of that on the
way home.*

Then, having done for the outlaws,
He shoved me out of the way
And had a go at Robin Hood.
That wasn't part of the play!

In my opinion, Miss Hodge should have stopped it then.

Now Kevin had this plastic sword
(The play was his idea)
And being who he was, of course,
Was supposed to show no fear.

I was showing fear, and Janek was on my side.

But once the sword was broke in half,
And minus his Merrie Men,
Robin Hood dropped the other half
And surrendered there and then.

Then Miss Hodge stopped it.

Anyway, that was the end of that.
The audience gave us a clap.
Me and Roy took the curtain down
And joined the rush for the tap.

It's thirsty work, acting; and we had our moustaches
to wash off.

Roy also fetched the first-aid box,
Put a plaster on his shin,
And offered to settle Kevin's nerves
With a junior aspirin.

Kevin was worried what his mum was going to say
about the sword.

Janek, meanwhile, was prowling round
With his sword still in his hand;
Suspecting another ambush, perhaps,
From another outlaw band.

Miss Hodge said he reminded her of Errol Flynn,
whoever he was.

Keith said, let's wait for the Christmas play
And have Janek in again.
He'd make mincemeat of the shepherds,
And slaughter the Three Wise Men.

He'd be worse than Herod, Keith said.

But I'm about fed up with plays;
Football's a better bet.
Now we've got this match against Class 4
And we've never beaten them yet.

You can probably guess what was in my mind;
Roy could.

So tomorrow Janek brings his kit
(The kick-off's half-past three);
And we'll play him in the forward line:
He's a striker . . . obviously.

The Mighty Slide

The snow has fallen in the night.
The temperature's exactly right.
The playground's ready, white and wide;
Just waiting for the mighty slide.

The first to arrive is Denis Dunne.
He takes a little stuttering run.
Sideways he slides across the snow;
He moves about a yard or so,
With knees just bent and arms out wide;
And marks the beginning of the slide.

Then Martin Bannister appears,
His collar up around his ears,
His zipper zipped, his laces tied,
And follows Denis down the slide.
The snow foams up around their feet,
And melts, too, in the friction's heat.
It changes once, it changes twice:
Snow to water; water to ice.

Now others arrive: the Fisher twins
And Alice Price. A queue begins.
The slide grows longer, front and back,
Like a giant high-speed snail's track.
And flatter and greyer and glassier too;
And as it grows, so does the queue.
Each waits in line and slides and then
Runs round and waits and slides again.

And little is said and nothing is planned,
As more and more children take a hand
(Or a foot, if you like) in the slide's construction.
They work without wages and minus instruction.
Like a team of cleaners to and fro
With clever feet they polish the snow.
Like a temporary tribe in wintry weather,
They blow on their gloves and pull together.

A dozen children, maybe more,
All skidding on the frozen floor.
The brave, like bulls, just charge the ice,
And one of these is Alice Price;
Her red scarf flying in the breeze,
You'd think she had a pair of skis.
Others approach more cautiously;
Denis for one (though he wouldn't agree).
His wobbly style is unmistakable:
The sign of a boy who knows he's breakable.

And now the slide is really growing,
And the rhythm of the queue is flowing.
Some keep a place or wait for a friend,
Some dive in the snow when they reach the end,
Some slide and pretend to be terrified,
Some stand in the queue and *never* slide.

There are children with bags and children without,
As they roll the silver carpet out;
And some in pairs and some in a bunch,
And one or two *eating*: an early lunch.
There's flying hair and frozen feet,
And big and little, and scruffy and neat.
There's shouting and shoving: 'Watch this!' 'Watch me!'
'I'm floating!' 'I'm falling!' 'Oh, Mother!' 'Wheee!'
And all the while from the frosty ground
That indescribable *sliding* sound.
Yes, snow's a pleasure and no mistake,
But the slide is the icing on the cake.

'If we knocked that wall down, moved that shed,
We could slide for miles!' the children said.
'If we knocked it *all* down – wallop – bop –
We could slide for ever and never stop!'
An icy ribbon tidily curled
In a giant circle round the world.

The slide by now is forty feet long,
And a number of things have begun to go wrong.
The queue stretches back to the playground gate;
Certain boys find it hard to wait.
While tough boys like Hoskins or Kenny Burns
Are simply not *used* to taking turns.
Like pockets of chaos or bits of sin,
They break up the queue and muscle in.

And all the time the slide gets slicker,
And the sliders slide along it quicker.
The quickest by far is Frankie Slater:
'When I grow up I'll be a skater!'
The craziest? Well, Colin Whittle;
He thinks the boy in front is a skittle.
There's bumps and bruises, bets and dares,
Cries, collisions, pile-ups, *prayers*.

But even worse than damaged kids,
The slide itself is on the skids.
The feet that brought it to perfection
Are pushing it now in a different direction.
For everything changes, that much is true;
And a part of the playground is poking through.

'It's wearing away! It's wearing out!
We need more snow!' the children shout.
At which point Hoskins quietly swears,
And – minus the coat he never wears –
Raises his hand like a traffic cop
And calls on his fellow sliders to stop.

Then straight away from the ranks of the queue
Step Denis and Martin and Alice too.
With no one to tell them and no one to ask,
They tackle the urgent chilly task.
They scoop the snow from either side
And bandage up the poorly slide.
Tread on it, trample it, smooth it, thump it.
'If that don't work, we'll have to jump it!'
'Jump what?' says Denis, looking queasy.
'The gap!' says Alice. 'Easy-peasy.'

Elsewhere in the playground, the usual scene:
A teacher on duty, it's Mrs Green.
A huddle of (mostly) shivering mums;
Some wondering babies, sucking thumbs
(Watching the world from way behind
As they wait in a queue of a different kind).
A gang of girls, they're shivering too,
Discussing who'll be friends with who.
A little infant darting about,
Giving his birthday invites out.
While scattered here and there besides,
Half a dozen smaller slides.
Snowball battles, snowball chases,
Swimming kit and violin cases:
A student with a tiger skin,
And *fourteen* children to carry it in.

The slide, meanwhile, with its cold compress,
Restored to health, well, more or less,
Remains by far the star attraction,
As Denis and Co. glide back into action.
With breath like smoke and cheeks like roses,
Pounding hearts and runny noses,
Eyes a-sparkle, nerves a-quiver,
Not a chance of a chill or a sign of a shiver
(It's a funny thought, that – it's nice – it's neat:
A thing made of ice and it generates heat),
They slide and queue and slide again;
There's six in a line – no, seven – no, ten!

A motley crew, a happy band,
Attending their own strip of land.
'Fifty foot long by two foot wide!'
'By half an inch thick!' – that's the mighty slide.
Cool and grey and, now, complete.
A work of art, all done by feet.

Then, suddenly, a whistle blows,
And all the human dynamos
(With outstretched arms and just-bent knees)
Skid to a halt, fall silent, freeze.
They stand in a trance, their hot breath steaming;
Rub their eyes as though they've been dreaming,
Or are caught in the bossy whistle's spell,
Or simply weary – it's hard to tell.
A few of them shiver, the air feels cool;
And the thought sinks in: it's time for school.

A little while later, observe the scene,
Transformed by a whistle and Mrs Green:
The empty playground, white and wide;
The scruffy snow, the silent slide.

Inside, with a maths card just begun
And his thoughts elsewhere, sits Denis Dunne.
His hands are chapped, his socks are wet,
But in his head he's sliding yet.
He sits near a window, he stares through the glass.
The teacher frowns from the front of the class.
Can this boy move! Can this boy skate!
'Come on, Denis – concentrate.'
Yes, nothing changes, that much is true,
And the chances of sliding in classrooms are few.
So Denis abandons his speculation,
And gets on with his education.

Some plough the land, some mow or mine it;
While others – if you let them – shine it.

The Famous Five-a-Side

The early morning sun beams bright
Into our uncle's cottage kitchen.
Uncle himself researches in his study,
Our parents are conveniently absent.

We breakfast well on eggs and toast
Get changed into our freshly laundered kit
Pick apples in the sunny orchard
Pack boots and buns and lemonade.

The village street is oddly quiet
Anxious faces at the bread-shop window.
There is a rumour of strange goings-on
Burglaries . . . a missing necklace.

The pitch upon the village green
Still sparkles with its morning dew
Except, that is, for one mysterious patch.
We fasten Timmy's dog-lead to a bench.

Descending from a battered van
The opposing team are not what we expect.
Older and scowling, oddly kitted out
Their goalie has an eye-patch and a beard.

The ref too has a sinister air
Arriving out of breath and with a limp.
He keeps the ball clutched closely to his chest
And seems unwilling to relax his grip.

'This lot aren't Barford Rovers, that's for sure,'
We whisper as we line up on the pitch.
Julian pretends to tie a bootlace up
And tells the rest of us he's got a plan.

The game begins. Their strategy is odd.
They crowd around the ball and hardly move.
The referee limps slowly up and down.
The bearded goalie smokes a cigarette.

Then suddenly we hear a sound
A hollow croaking voice *beneath* the grass.
A trap door in the turf begins to rise
And reaching up around it comes . . . a hand!

George boots the ball now high into the air
It ends up in the smoking goalie's net.
His team mates oddly chase it in,
The hobbling referee not far behind.

'This is our chance, chaps!' Julian cries.
We charge then at the crowded goal,
Unhook the net and drop it on them all:
The spurious players and the bogus ref.

Meanwhile up from his dungeon cell
One plain-clothes CID man stumbles forth.
'Well done, you fellows – excellent!' he gasps.
(This was more 'undercover' than he'd planned.)

'This is the Melford Mob,' he says.
'Been on their trail all year.
I shouldn't doubt there'll be a big reward.'
'We *knew* they were suspicious,' George declares.

Another van appears: the Black Maria.
The losing side are bundled in.
'You blasted kids!' the captured goalie growls.
Brave Timmy barks as they are driven off.

That little dog now trots towards the ball,
He sniffs and scrabbles at it with his paws.
'He wants to tell us something,' Anne explains.
Yes – have you guessed? – the *necklace* was inside.

Back home to Uncle's cottage, time for lunch.
There's sausages and chocolate cake and squash.
'Good game?' says Uncle, peering round the door.
'Oh absolutely yes!' cries George. 'We won!'

Dog in the Playground

Dog in the playground
Suddenly there.
Smile on his face,
Tail in the air.

Dog in the playground
Bit of a fuss:
I know that dog –
Lives next to us!

Dog in the playground:
Oh, no he don't.
He'll come with me,
You see if he won't.

The word gets round;
The crowd gets bigger.
His name's Bob.
It ain't – it's Trigger.

They call him Archie!
They call him Frank!
Lives by the Fish Shop!
Lives up the Bank!
Who told you that?
Pipe down! Shut up!
I know that dog
Since he was a pup.

Dog in the playground:
We'll catch him, Miss.
Leave it to us.
Just watch this!

Dog in the playground
What a to-do!
Thirty-five children,
Caretaker too,
Chasing the dog,
Chasing each other.
I know that dog –
He's our dog's brother!

We've cornered him now;
He can't get away.
Told you we'd catch him,
Robert and – Hey!
Don't open that door –
Oh, Glenis, you fool!
Look, Miss, what's happened:
Dog in the school.

Dog in the classroom,
Dog in the hall,
Dog in the toilets –
He's paying a call!
Forty-six children,
Caretaker too,
Headmaster, three teachers,
Hullabaloo!

Lost him! Can't find him!
He's vanished! And then:
Look, Miss, he's back
In the playground again.

Shouting and shoving –
I'll give you what for! –
Sixty-five children
Head for the door.

Dog in the playground,
Smile on his face,
Tail in the air,
Winning the race.

Dog in his element
Off at a jog,
Out of the gates:
Wish I was a dog.

Dog in the playground:
Couldn't he run?

Dog in the playground
         . . . Gone!

The Match (c. 1950)

The match was played in Albert Park
From half-past four till after dark
By two opposing tribes of boys
Who specialized in mud and noise;

Scratches got from climbing trees
Runny noses, scabby knees
Hair shaved halfway up the head
And names like Horace, Archie, Ted.

The match was played come rain or shine
By boys who you could not confine
Whose common goals all unconcealed
Were played out on the football field.

Off from school in all directions
Sparks of boys with bright complexions
Rushing home with one idea
To grab their boots . . . and disappear.

But Mother in the doorway leaning
Brings to this scene a different meaning
The jobs and duties of a son
Yes, there are *errands to be run*.

Take this wool to Mrs Draper
Stop at Pollock's for a paper
Mind this baby, beat this rug
Give your poor old mum a hug.

Eat this apple, eat this cake
Eat these dumplings, carrots, steak!
Bread 'n' drippin', bread 'n' jam
Mind the traffic, so long, scram.

Picture this, you're gazing down
Upon that smoky factory town.
Weaves of streets spread out, converge
And from the houses boys emerge.

Specks of boys, a broad selection
Heading off in one direction
Pulled by some magnetic itch
Up to the park, on to the pitch.

Boys in boots and boys in wellies
Skinny boys and boys with bellies
Tiny boys with untied laces
Brainy boys with violin cases.

The match was played to certain rules
By boys from certain streets and schools
Who since their babyhood had known
Which patch of earth to call their own.

The pitch, meanwhile, you'd have to say
Was nothing, just a place to play.
No nets, no posts, no *lines*, alas
The only thing it had was grass.

Each team would somehow pick itself
No boys were left upon the shelf
No substitutions, sulks or shame
If you showed up, you got a game.

Not 2·3·5 or 4·2·4
But 2·8·12 or even more.
Six centre forwards, five right wings
Was just the normal run of things.

Lined up then in such formations
Careless of life's complications
Deaf to birdsong, blind to flowers
Prepared to chase a ball for hours,

A swarm of boys who heart and soul
Must make a bee-line for the goal.
A kind of ordered anarchy
(There was, of course, *no* referee).

They ran and shouted, ran and shot
(At passing they were not so hot)
Pulled a sock up, rolled a sleeve
And scored more goals than you'd believe.

Slid and tackled, leapt and fell
Dodged and dribbled, dived as well
Headed, shouldered, elbowed, kneed
And, half-time in the bushes, peed.

With muddy shorts and muddy faces
Bloody knees and busted laces
Ruddy cheeks and plastered hair
And voices buffeting the air.

Voices flung above the trees
Heard half a mile away with ease,
For every throw in, every kick
Required an inquest double quick.

A shouting match, all fuss and fury
(Prosecutors, judges, jury)
A match of mouths set to repeat
The main and muddier match of feet.

Thus hot and bothered, loud and nifty
That's how we played in 1950
A maze of moves, a fugue of noise
From forty little boiling boys.

Yet there was talent, don't forget
Grace and courage too, you bet
Boys like Briggs or Tommy Gray
Who were, quite simply, *born* to play.

You could have stuck them on the moon
They would have started scoring soon
No swanky kit, uncoached, unheeded
A pumped-up ball was all they needed.

Around the fringes of the match
Spectators to this hectic patch
Younger sisters, older brothers
Tied-up dogs and irate mothers.

A mother come to claim her twins
(Required to *play* those violins).
A little sister, Annabelle,
Bribed with a lolly not to tell.

Dogs named Rover, Rex or Roy
Each watching one particular boy.
A pup mad keen to chase the ball
The older dogs had seen it all.

The match was played till after dark
(Till gates were closed on Albert Park)
By shadowy boys whose shapes dissolved
Into the earth as it revolved.

Ghostly boys who flitted by
Like bats across the evening sky,
A final fling, a final call
Pursuing the invisible ball.

The match was played, the match *is* over
For Horace, Annabelle and Rover.
A multitude of feet retrace
The steps that brought them to this place.

For gangs of neighbours, brothers, friends
A slow walk home is how it ends,
Into a kitchen's steamy muddle
To get a shouting at . . . or cuddle.

See it now, you're looking down
Upon that lamp-lit factory town.
It's late (it's *night*) for Rex or Ted
And everybody's gone to bed.

Under the rooftops slicked with rain
The match is being played again
By two opposing well-scrubbed teams
Who race and holler in their dreams.

Glen Hills
Primary School
Featherby Drive
Glen Parva
March 16th 1988

Dear Allan for reading us the stories
Thank you
I like the JOLLY POSTMAN
and I like Mr Biff the Boxer
as well on book week we dressed
up and I dressed up as the
Pied Piper and Kelly dressed up as
mary mary quite coherary and we made
a Play

Love from
Elliot
xxxxxxx
xxxxxxxx
xxxx/x

7th December

A very big thank you to mr Ahberg
For sending us a letter. I loved it . It
was the best one I had in a long time.
In school we are making costumes
for are school play. It is fun. I cant wait
untill you come to our school. you are the best
Poet I have ever been doing a poem to. Are school
Play is the Jesse tree.

Best wishes
emily xx

AFTER WORDS

If you write children's books, one bonus is you get children's *letters*, generous letters that conclude, often as not, with love and kisses. Letters, in my case, that praise me for my 'poems', promote me to a poet. Well, there could be a poem in here, somewhere, but I suspect it's mostly light verse. Yet there it is on the cover, 'Collected Poems'. For children, if it rhymes or sits on the page in short lines, it's a poem. Verse rarely gets a mention . . . which I thought I'd mention.

The poems/verses here have been sifted from five books written over a period of twenty-five years. I have not included picture-book texts, *Each Peach Pear Plum*, for instance, or *Cops and Robbers*. Somehow they were just too wrapped up in and around Janet's pictures. Excluded also are a number of more recent efforts, although this one nearly got in:

> Uncle Edith
> This poem, I regret to say,
> Is quite untrue.
> Uncle was really Auntie, of course,
> And Edith, actually, Hugh.

I wish to thank the Superintendent of Parks and Cemeteries for Oldbury in the 1960s, Mr McGibbon. I was employed then, in one of his cemeteries, as a gravedigger. Eventually, Mr McGibbon persuaded me up and out of my hole in the ground and propelled me off to become, in the fullness of time, a teacher. Mr McGibbon was my Good Samaritan. I owe him.

Yes, and Harry and Dennis too, my fellow gravediggers, who taught me that all work has its skills. The graves they dug were ten feet deep, neat and perpendicular and coffin-shaped. They did not move one spadeful of earth more than was needed (mitred corners, tapered ends). My graves, ragged-edged and sloping, were not a patch on theirs. The digging I do now is with a pen. It is a trade – prose, poetry or verse – I'm better suited for. No dog with a bone, but a treasure-hunter, maybe. Love and kisses.

A. A.

Bath, 2008

INDEX OF FIRST LINES

We have, it seems, a few spare pages here. It's a shame to waste them. So here's one more – a bonus track.

Having a Baby

I came from Battersea
In 1938
Delivered by a steam train
Forty minutes late.

(Not the Dogs' Home, though.)

My mother went to fetch me
By tram, then train
With Dad, as usual, working:
Hope's – Window Frames.

(Or was it Danks's Boilers?)

My mother had a shopping bag:
Bootees, bottle, shawl
And knitting for the journey
Not much else at all.

(A purse, I suppose; hat, glasses and such.)

She struggled across London
Got lost near Waterloo
And came at last to the Orphanage
At twenty-five to two.

(Early, even so, for a two o'clock appointment.)

They sat her in the corridor
Left her there till three
Then gave her a couple of documents,
A form to sign – and me.

(She couldn't see to write. 'M'glasses needed wipers!')

Back then to Paddington
Weather wet and mild
Brand-new mother
Second-hand child.

(Good condition, though; one previous owner.)

And Mother clutched her secret
On her lap
From all the other passengers
All the way back.

(Dad, still in his overalls, was on the platform.)

He squeezed us in a cuddle
Gave me a clumsy kiss
He smelled of wood-shavings and oil
Mum specially remembered this.

(And me? Asleep, apparently. I'd had a busy day.)

For my parents
GEORGE AND ELIZABETH AHLBERG
who gave me a home, and kept me out of one.

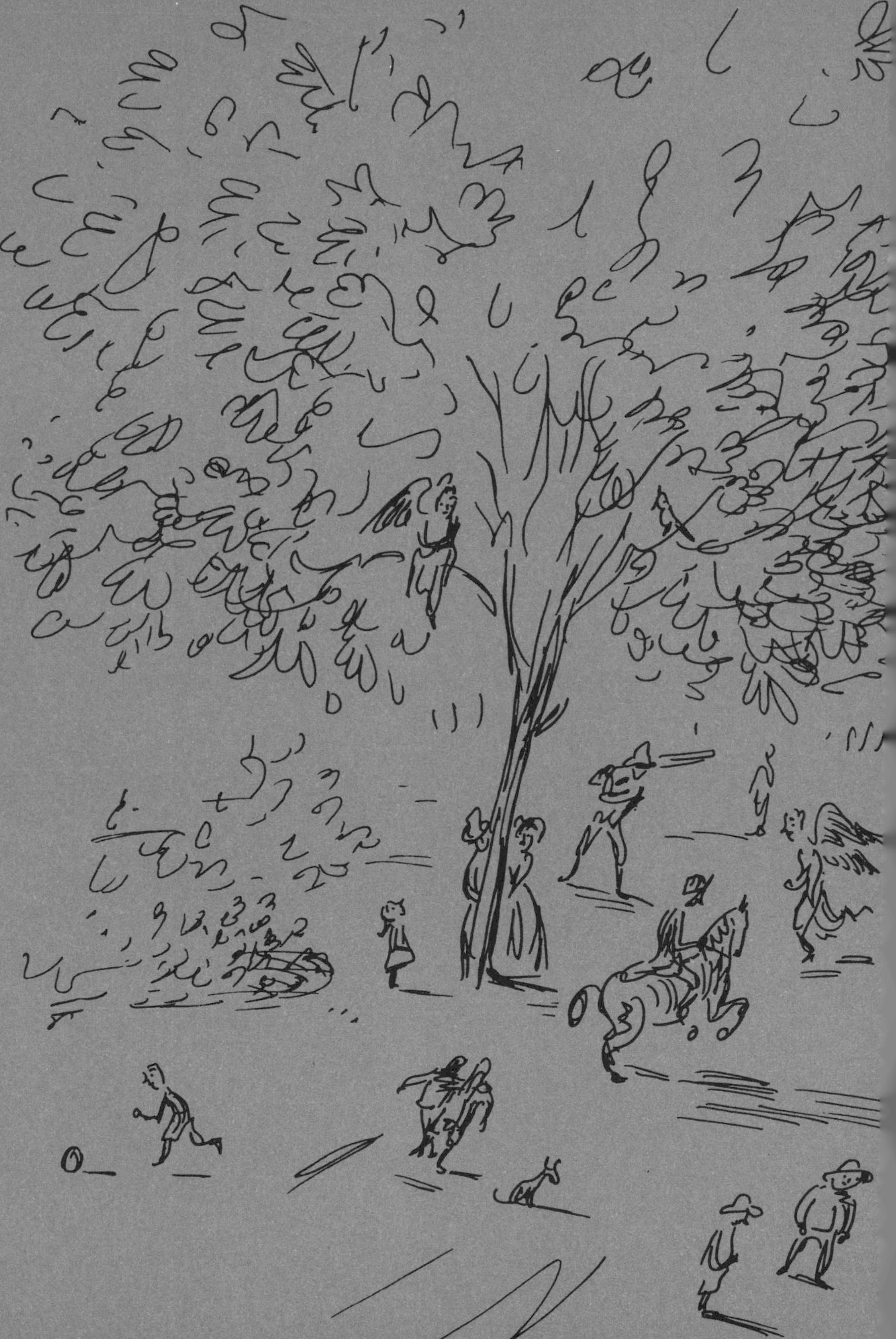